Harumi's Japanese Home Cooking

Harumi Kurihara

A HOME BOOK
Published by the Penguin Group
Penguin Group (USA) Inc.
375 Hudson Street, New York, New York 10014, USA

Penguin Group (Canada), 90 Eglinton Avenue East, Suite 700, Toronto, Ontario M4P 2Y3, Canada (a division of Pearson Penguin Canada Inc.) • Penguin Books Ltd., 80 Strand, London WC2RoRL, England • Penguin Group Ireland, 25 St. Stephen's Green, Dublin 2, Ireland (a division of Penguin Books Ltd.) • Penguin Group (Australia), 250 Camberwell Road, Camberwell, Victoria 3124, Australia (a division of Pearson Australia Group Pty. Ltd.) • Penguin Books India Pvt. Ltd., 11 Community Centre, Panchsheel Park, New Dehli—110 017, India • Penguin Group (NZ), 67 Apollo Drive, Rosedale, North Shore 0745, Auckland, New Zealand (a division of Pearson New Zealand Ltd.) • Penguin Books (South Africa) (Pty.) Ltd., 24 Sturdee Avenue, Rosebank, Johannesburg 2196, South Africa

Penguin Books Ltd., Registered Offices: 80 Strand, London WC2R oRL, England

HARUMI'S JAPANESE HOME COOKING

Recipes copyright © by Harumi Kurihara

Text copyright © by Harumi Kurihara and FCI London 2006
Photography copyright © by Fusosha Inc.

Text Harumi Kurihara and Sue Hudson
Editor Akiko Sakaguchi (Japan)
Translation Tomoko Miyakoda
Project coordination Sue Hudson, Akiko Sakaguchi and Tomoko Miyakoda
Publishing Director Lorraine Dickey
Editor Sybella Marlow
Contributing Editor Shirley Booth
Art Director Jonathan Christie
Original Design Concept Mark Thomson
Production Controller Jane Rogers
Photo Research Hanako Itahashi and Miho Yoshinari
Special Thanks Yutaka Seino and Nobuko Suzuki

Photo credits
Lisa Linder pp 5, 8, 12, 13, 14, 15, 17, 152
Takeharu Hioki pp 72, 90, 91, 99, 134, 135
Takahiro Imashimizu pp 13, 42, 46, 56, 57, 58, 59, 92, 110, 112, 115, 116, 117, 157
Masao Kudo pp 14, 16, 18, 20, 34, 35, 36, 38, 39, 41, 47, 48, 49, 62, 66, 67, 76, 77, 80, 81, 84, 85, 86, 87, 91, 107, 108, 120, 121, 124, 125, 126, 127, 129, 136, 137, 143, 144, 145, 146, 147, 155
Teruaki Nagamine pp 26, 27, 98
Hiroyasu Nakano pp 18, 25, 60, 88, 90, 91, 130, 131, 140, 148, 152, 153, 154, 157
Kazuaki Nakazato pp 24, 45, 60, 63, 70, 71, 100, 101, 106, 118, 119
Takeshi Noguchi pp 68, 69, 88, 110, 149
Akio Takeuchi pp 2, 11, 19, 21, 23, 28, 29, 30, 31, 33, 40, 43, 50, 51, 52, 53, 54, 55, 61, 64, 65, 73, 75, 78, 79, 82, 83, 89, 93, 95, 96, 102, 103, 104, 105, 109, 111, 114, 122, 123, 128, 132, 133, 138, 139, 142, 147, 148, 151, 152, 155, 156

First American edition: October 2007
Previously published in Great Britain in 2006 by Conran Octopus Limited.
All recipes published in Fusosha's Kurihara Harumi's Suteki Recipe in Japan.

Home hardcover ISBN: 978-1-55788-520-3

PRINTED IN CHINA

10 9 8 7 6 5 4 3

PUBLISHER'S NOTE: The recipes contained in this book are to be followed exactly as written. The publisher is not responsible for your specific health or allergy needs that may require medical supervision. The publisher is not responsible for any adverse reactions to the recipes contained in this book.

Most Home Books are available at special quantity discounts for bulk purchases for sales promotions, premiums, fundraising, or educational use. Special books, or book excerpts, can also be created to fit specific needs. For details, write: Special Markets, Penguin Group (USA) Inc., 375 Hudson Street, New York, New York 10014.

Harumi's Japanese Home Cooking

Harumi Kurihara

"I hope I have helped people to find the real pleasure and creativity that there is in cooking and eating."

Contents

Please call me Harumi...

Life for me has changed dramatically since the publication of my book *Harumi's Japanese Cooking*. I have traveled the world meeting people, talking about Japanese food and showing people just how easy it is to cook it outside Japan. I would like to think that my recipes are helping to build links between my native Japan and the rest of the world.

Winning the Gourmand World Cookbook Award and having my book published internationally has also strengthened my resolve to try to improve my schoolgirl's English. Like many other Japanese people, I studied English at school but never imagined using it. Now I am finding that times have changed and I must change, too.

I have recently taken part in a Japanese television series about learning English. For the program I have to speak English in different imaginary situations, and one of the first episodes is about being at a party with lots of English-speaking people. I have to go up to people at the party and introduce myself—a nerve-wracking thing even in my own language, let alone in English. My line is "Hello, my name is Harumi Kurihara, but please call me Harumi . . ." It feels a little alien and rather intimate to use my first name like this but I have to remember that many people overseas use their first names rather than their family names. It is part of the many cultural differences between Japan and the rest of the world that make life interesting.

In Japan people usually call me by my family name or by the word *sensei*, which means "teacher." It feels strange for me to be called this—as I have always seen myself as just a regular Japanese housewife. If you had told me when I first married that this would be my future, I would not have believed you. Even now I sometimes have to pinch myself to check that I am not dreaming!

Ever since Harumi's Japanese Cooking was published my life has become ridiculously busy. I feel that I am cramming two days' work into each day, but at the same time I try to ensure that I have a fairly normal family life. I still get up early, prepare offerings for the family shrine, feed the cats and water the garden, after which my husband and I have breakfast together. I prepare the food and he makes the tea. This time is so precious for us, when we can chat on our own and enjoy being together.

Cookbook writing and the design work I do have occurred as a result of happy accidents rather than a planned career. My work has really originated from my being a housewife and mother and from being lucky enough to have a family who has encouraged me every step of the way. Most women of my generation have never worked outside their homes; I have been very fortunate to have had such support and understanding.

My husband, Reiji, has been a huge influence on me in many ways. He has always had very sophisticated and international tastes and encouraged me to try different cuisines and ingredients. He worked in the Japanese media and often brought friends home for dinner. As a result, I was asked to help with a cooking segment on television; this then became a regular slot and led to cooking columns and then a book, Gochiso Sama Ga Kikitakute (I Want to Hear That Was Delicious), and a quarterly magazine, Suteki Recipes (Lovely Recipes), which really marked the beginning of my work. I am fortunate to have had many cookbooks and magazines published in Japan and I hope I have helped my readers to find the pleasure and creativity in cooking.

Most of my readers are women but I write for men, too. The reality of modern Japan is that it is mainly women who do the daily cooking but I hope men will also enjoy my recipes.

When I was first approached to write a Japanese cookbook for the Western market, I was not sure whether there would be sufficient interest for it to be successful. I spent time selecting recipes that could be made with few specialty ingredients and suggested substitutions in the hope that it would encourage people to try a different way of cooking.

When I came overseas to promote Harumi's Japanese Cooking I had a lot of fun teaching people how to make Inside-Out Sushi and talking about Japanese food. One question that frequently cropped up was, "Which pieces of Japanese kitchen equipment do you think are essential?" It started me thinking about cooking as more than just ingredients and about how cultural differences appear in so many unexpected ways.

In addition to rice cookers, which you can now find almost everywhere, I decided that the following pieces of equipment are the most useful and have the greatest effect on Japanese cooking: knives, chopsticks, graters, drop lids and a grooved mortar and pestle.

Japanese Cooking Techniques

Knives Hocho

Japanese knives are justifiably internationally renowned. We have a long history of making swords and these same skills are used in the making of knives. I think some Japanese chefs love their knives as if they were human! If you go to look for a knife, you will be amazed at the range and the cost. You could spend a fortune on just one knife. Traditionally, knives were made from steel but they require a lot of maintenance to keep them sharp and usable. These days, many everyday cooks, like myself, find it easier to use stainless steel knives.

I use many types of knives, selecting the most suitable one for each ingredient, but I find I mainly use one about 12 inches long for daily use and another small paring one. It is important, however, that any knife you use is kept very sharp.

Those readers who bought Harumi's Japanese Cooking will recall that I wrote that I am very pragmatic about ingredients in my recipes but not so relaxed about how ingredients, particularly vegetables, are prepared for each dish. When you learn to cook in Japan you are taught how to use many different cutting styles, which in turn affects how food looks and tastes. You can even buy whole books dedicated to showing cutting styles for different ingredients. I think this indicates how seriously we take the subject. The Japanese language, too, has a series of words to indicate how things are cut. It is interesting for me to see how relatively clumsy English as a language is for these words.

The most common styles of cutting are:

Mijingiri finely minced (into tiny cube shapes)
Sengiri julienned or into strips
Hangetsugiri cut into half moons
Koguchigiri cut into fine slices—for round ingredients like spring onions
Nanamegiri cut on the diagonal
Ichogiri round pieces cut into quarters
Usugiri finely sliced

I believe flavors of ingredients change according to the cutting style you use. As an experiment, try to cut and use an ingredient like garlic in the following ways and see how differently it tastes: usugiri (thinly sliced), sengiri (cut into fine strips), mijingiri (minced), tsubusu (squashed) or orosu (grated). It is an interesting exercise and worth trying.

I wanted to introduce the importance of cutting in this book, as I feel it is a valuable part of Japanese cooking and perhaps one of the few things I feel you need to do correctly. For example, for most Japanese it would be unthinkable to have Tonkatsu (see page 66) without a mountain of finely shredded cabbage—quick and easy to prepare once you have learned how to do it. Similarly, it would be impossible to incorporate onion into a Teriyaki Hamburger without it being finely minced; try not to cut the onion right to the root end, as this allows you to get a much finer cut.

Chopsticks & Cooking Chopsticks Hashi & Saibashi

As I mentioned earlier, I had never really stopped to think about what equipment I use in the kitchen; I just use it. But when I was asked I suddenly realized that many other countries don't do things the way we do in Japan. I don't even think about how I am using some things like cooking chopsticks—they are so integral to life in the kitchen that they feel like second nature.

What are cooking chopsticks? Well, they are longer than the chopsticks we use to eat with and most houses have a minimum of 3 pairs in use at the same time. Like chopsticks that are used for eating, they give the sense of having long fingers—such is the intimacy they effect.

You can use cooking chopsticks to cook anything in a wok, and deep frying can be easily dealt with, too. You can turn over thinly

sliced meat or fish more easily with cooking chopsticks; you can even clean oil out of pans by using chopsticks and paper towels. You can mix ingredients together and delicately arrange food on serving dishes, too, with these chopsticks. Once you have started to use them you will never look back—so easy but also so responsive to the various stages of cooking. They also take up very little room compared to equipment like tongs.

I would like to tell you a little about the different chopsticks that exist in Asia. In general, Chinese chopsticks tend to be slightly longer than Japanese ones. They are often rectangular rather than round and they do not usually have the pointed end that is typical of Japanese chopsticks. In contrast to the Japanese lacquer or wood or the Chinese ivory or wood, the Koreans often have chopsticks that are made of metal but are of a similar design to Japanese ones.

If you have always wondered about how to hold them correctly, I would like to assure you that it is fairly simple. One chopstick should rest on your ring finger with its end resting in the V between your thumb and index finger. The other is held between the thumb, index and middle fingers. You should be able to move the chopstick that is held by the thumb, index, and middle fingers independently of the other one. Practice will make it easier! Once you have mastered chopsticks you will be amazed at how natural they feel—I think you have a closer relationship with your food using them.

In addition to the lacquer chopsticks we use at home, we also use disposable chopsticks in restaurants. These plain wooden chopsticks come in pairs and are designed to be split into two for use. We also have serving chopsticks (toribashi), which are longer than the ones we use for eating but shorter than the ones used for cooking. Again they are really useful and responsive to use. If there are no serving chopsticks you can pick up food from a communal plate using the end of your chopsticks that has not been in your mouth.

One final point: it is not considered good manners to leave your chopsticks in your food. Leave them across the top of a bowl or across the edge of a plate but not in the bowl or plate.

Ginger Graters Shoga oroshi **and other graters**

The graters commonly used in Japan are not like graters in Western countries. Instead of cutting through ingredients, Japanese graters almost pulp them. They are usually made of ceramic or metal but if you have the chance to use a traditional wasabi (Japanese horseradish) grater, you will be very surprised to find that it is made of shark skin.

Graters are mainly used for wasabi, garlic, ginger and daikon (Japanese mooli) and size differs according to use. I like to put a small ginger grater on the table so everyone can grate their own to add to their meal. If you go to any Japanese restaurant you will have seen little mounds of grated daikon—it is commonly served with tempura or grilled fish. As I mentioned earlier, how you deal with vegetables affects the taste and, for tempura, grilled and fried dishes, daikon must be grated to a pulp, not chopped.

These graters are not so easy to find outside Japan (though I believe you might find something similar in France for garlic grating) but they are certainly worth buying if you can find them. They give a particular flavor to your food that doesn't come from an ordinary grater.

Drop Lids Otoshibuta

Traditionally, drop lids were made of wood. They are placed in a pan, directly on top of food as it cooks. It is a technique frequently used in Japanese cooking to ensure the even distribution of flavor. These days, most households use lids made of aluminum foil or greaseproof paper with a hole in the middle. You can fashion a disk easily, making sure it is slightly smaller than the inside of the pan. It is a different way of cooking but it is very useful and very Japanese.

Japanese mortar and pestle Suribachi

Many Japanese recipes include sesame in some form or another—particularly as a sauce. Traditionally, we make this by grinding toasted sesame seeds in a suribachi until they become a paste. A suribachi is a Japanese mortar and pestle that is grooved on the inside, allowing more friction and so enabling a cook to turn the seeds into a paste. They come in all sorts of different sizes and the pestle is usually made of wood.

In my kitchenware range, I have designed my own suribachi because I like to use it as a serving dish too. For example, in Harumi's Japanese Cooking, I included a recipe for vegetables with a black sesame dressing in which I like to make the dressing in the suribachi and then stir in the lightly cooked vegetables. It looks great and ensures that all the dressing is effectively used.

I hope that you will take up the challenge and try to prepare these recipes using some of this equipment. I believe that it will create a different mood in your kitchen and this will influence your food. Through the creation of a delicious meal you can experience another culture—my culture, that of Japan.

Soup, Eggs & Tofu

Miso Soup with Tofu and Wakame Seaweed

Miso Shiru

This soup is a classic that many of you will have had in Japanese restaurants. It is easy to make, delicious and very healthy. You can serve it at any mealtime, and over the next few pages you will see that it also forms the basis of many other tasty soups.

SERVES 4

3¹/₂ cups dashi stock or fish stock

4 tablespoons awase miso paste (see Ingredients Note on page 21)

8-inch piece dried wakame seaweed

5 ounces soft/silken tofu

finely chopped spring onions—to garnish

For the dashi stock:

5 cups water

3¹/₂ tablespoons dried fish flakes (katsuo bushi— shavings of dried bonito/tuna fish)

1 Heat the dashi stock in a saucepan. Just before it comes to a boil, add the miso and stir until completely dissolved.

2 Soak the wakame seaweed in water until soft. Drain and cut into bite-size pieces.

3 Hold the tofu in your hand and cut into ¹/₂-inch square pieces (see photos). Add first the tofu, then the wakame seaweed to the soup. Heat thoroughly, taking care not to let it boil. Garnish with finely chopped spring onions.

To make dashi stock

Heat the water and just before it comes to a boil, add the dried fish flakes and simmer for 1–2 minutes over low heat. Turn off the heat and leave the fish flakes to sink to the bottom of the pan, then strain. You can reuse these flakes to make a weaker dashi. Any remaining dashi stock can be frozen.

Miso Soup with Eggplant

In Japan, this delicious soup is popular in autumn when komatsuna is at its best.

SERVES 2

¹/₄ cup eggplant
¹/₄ cup komatsuna or spinach
1³/₄ cups dashi stock or fish stock
2¹/₂ tablespoons awase miso paste
chili powder or shichimi togarashi—to taste

Ingredients Note

Miso is a paste made from fermented soybeans and rice or barley. As it is considered to be so good for you, it can be found outside Japan in many health food shops. There are 3 basic types of miso: red (aka miso), which is dark and high in salt; white (shiro miso), which is paler and tends to be sweet; and mixed miso (awase miso), which is best for this classic soup. Mix the miso to a thin paste with a little of the hot stock before adding to the soup. Miso has a delicate aroma that is destroyed by boiling, so be careful not to boil the soup after adding the miso.

Instant dashi stock: if you are in a hurry or you cannot find the dried fish flakes (katsuo bushi), instant dashi stock is a good substitute.

1 Cut the eggplant into ¹/₂-inch-thick bite-size pieces and soak in cold water for about 5 minutes then boil to remove any bitterness.
2 When it has just softened, drain and soak in cold water until cool. Drain again.
3 Cut the komatsuna into 1-inch pieces.
4 Warm the dashi stock in a small pan, add the miso paste and stir until dissolved. Add the eggplant and komatsuna, simmer briefly and serve sprinkled with chili powder or shichimi togarashi.

Harumi's Hint

You can use a spoon to eat all these soups, but the traditional Japanese-style method is to drink the soup directly from the bowl using chopsticks for the chunks.

Miso Soup with Wakame Seaweed and Potato

You can serve this soup all year round. It is a good variation on the classic miso shiru.

SERVES 4

$^1\!/_2$ cup new potatoes

8-inch piece dried wakame seaweed

$3^1\!/_2$ cups dashi stock or fish stock

3–4 tablespoons awase miso paste

a few sprigs of kinome, if available, or thinly sliced spring onion—to garnish

Harumi's Hint

Another popular variation of miso shiru is my sesame-flavored miso soup. You can make this by adding half the amount of sesame paste to the amount of miso paste used (e.g., 3/4 tablespoon of sesame paste to every $1^1\!/_2$ tablespoons of miso paste). If you cannot find sesame paste you can use either unsweetened smooth peanut butter or tahini. This sesame paste soup is really delicious and very popular with my friends and family.

1 Peel the potatoes, halve them and cut into $^1\!/_2$-inch-thick semicircular pieces.

2 Soak the potatoes in water for about 5–6 minutes to remove the starch, then drain. Soak the dried wakame seaweed in water until soft. Drain and cut into bite-size pieces.

3 Bring the dashi stock to a boil, add the potatoes and simmer until they are just cooked. Add the miso paste and stir until dissolved. Do not bring back to a boil.

4 To serve, place a little wakame seaweed in each bowl, add the hot miso soup and garnish with kinome or spring onion.

Miso Soup with Pork

Tonjiru

This traditional soup is more like a stew and makes a lovely lunch dish. If you have a few vegetables you want to use up, you can easily include them in this recipe.

SERVES 4
1/2 lb. finely sliced pork
1 tablespoon sake
1 teaspoon soy sauce
1/2 cup potatoes
1 cup soft/silken tofu
1/4 cup spring onions
3 1/2 cups water
4–5 tablespoons awase miso paste
chili powder or shichimi togarashi—to taste

Ingredients Note
Shichimi togarashi is a frequently used mix of seven spices, which includes sansho (a Japanese pepper) and black sesame, but the overriding flavor is always chili.

Menu Planning
This soup makes a quick lunch, served with a bowl of rice and pickles. Or, for a more substantial meal, you can serve it with a fish dish such as the Grilled Salmon "Yuan" Style (see page 108).

1 Cut the pork into bite-size pieces and marinate in the sake and soy sauce.
2 Peel the potatoes and cut into 3/4- to 1-inch square pieces. Soak in cold water for about 5–6 minutes to remove starch, then drain.
3 Cut the tofu into 1/2- to 3/4-inch square pieces and thinly slice the spring onions on the diagonal.
4 In a pan, bring the water to a boil and add the pork. Skim off any fat from the surface, then add the potatoes and simmer until they are just cooked.
5 Add the tofu and spring onions, bring to a boil again, then turn off the heat. Add the miso paste, blending thoroughly.
Serve with a sprinkle of chili powder or shichimi togarashi.

Carrot and Miso Soup

Anyone who knows me will tell you that I love carrots; their color is so warming, especially in winter. The secret ingredient in this soup is miso, giving it a deeper flavor and added health benefits.

SERVES 2

1/3 cup carrots
13/4 cups water
1 chicken bouillon cube or 2 teaspoons granulated
   chicken stock powder
1 slice well-marbled bacon
1 tablespoon olive oil
2 tablespoons finely chopped celery
1/2 teaspoon awase miso
salt and pepper
chopped coriander—to garnish

1 Peel the carrots and cut into 1-inch-thick round slices.
2 Put the water and bouillon cube (crumbled) or powder
in a pan and bring to a boil. Then add the carrots and cover with a
drop lid. Turn down the heat and simmer until cooked. Remove
from heat and mash the cooked carrots in the remaining liquid.
3 Cut the bacon into small pieces. In a frying pan, heat the oil
and cook the chopped bacon until crispy. Turn the heat off and
mix in the chopped celery. Add to the carrot soup.
4 Bring to a boil then turn off the heat, mix in the miso and
season with salt and pepper.
5 Pour into bowls, sprinkle with coriander and serve.

Harumi's Hint

If you do not have a drop lid, you can make one
using a circle of foil or wax paper. Make the lid
small enough to fit inside the pan, so it can sit on
top of the cooking food (see page 16).

Mini Savory Steamed Egg Custards with Mushrooms

Kinoko no Chawan Mushi

This is my own simple version of the traditional Japanese savory steamed egg custard—chawan mushi. Usually small pieces of chicken, shrimp and vegetables are added, too, but here I use only nameko mushrooms. Also, although not traditional, I think this sauce really complements the chawan mushi.

SERVES 4

For the savory steamed egg custards:

1 teaspoon Chinese soup paste or a mix of chicken and beef stock

3/4 cup hot water

2 eggs

1 1/3 cups nameko, enoki or button mushrooms (chopped)

1/2 cup chopped spring onions or chives— to garnish

For the sauce:

a little granulated chicken stock powder

2 tablespoons hot water

1 tablespoon soy sauce

1/2 tablespoon rice vinegar

1 teaspoon sesame oil

a little chili oil (la-yu)—to taste

Menu Planning

Chawan mushi is great as a small side dish. It works very well with all Japanese dishes, but goes particularly well with strong-flavored recipes like Poached Red Sea Bream (see page 106) or Quick-Fried Steak (see page 82).

1   To make the custards: In a bowl, dissolve the Chinese soup paste in the hot water and leave for a few minutes until cool. In another bowl beat the eggs, add the stock, then mix well and strain through a sieve to remove any stringy bits.

2   Divide the mushrooms between 4 small cups and pour the egg stock on top.

3   To steam: In a steamer bring some water to a boil. Turn down the heat and place the dishes in the steamer. Cover with a tea towel and then with the lid, and steam for 12–15 minutes until cooked. The custard should be firm to the touch.

4   Make the sauce by dissolving the chicken stock powder in the hot water, then mix in the other ingredients until blended.

5   When the custards are ready, remove from the steamer and pour a little of the sauce onto each one. Garnish liberally with the spring onions or chives. Serve piping hot and eat with a spoon.

Clear Soup with Pork and Spinach Wonton Dumplings

This soup has a very strong Chinese accent. I like to serve it with other Chinese-influenced dishes like fried rice or Tofu with Spicy Minced Topping (see page 41).

SERVES 4

For the soup:

8 chicken wing tips

5 cups water

1^1/$_2$ cups spring onions (green parts only)

1 tablespoon fresh ginger, crushed

2 tablespoons sake

2 tablespoons soy sauce

1 tablespoon shokoshu or dry sherry

salt and pepper

coriander—to garnish

chili oil (la-yu)—to serve

For the wonton dumplings (makes 24):

3/4 cup spinach

1/4 lb. minced pork

Chinese soup paste or chicken bouillon cube/
    granules dissolved in 1 tablespoon hot water

2 teaspoons sesame oil

1 teaspoon soy sauce

1/2 teaspoon shokoshu or dry sherry

salt and pepper

2 teaspoons finely chopped ginger

12 wonton sheets

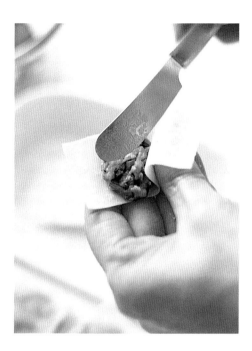

Ingredients Note

Shokoshu is a Chinese sake that has a stronger taste than Japanese sake. If you cannot find any, you can use dry sherry instead.

1 To make the soup: Thoroughly wash the chicken wings then pat dry. In a pan, bring the water to a boil and add the chicken, spring onions, crushed ginger and sake. Bring back to a boil and skim the surface before simmering for about 15 minutes. Drain the liquid into another pan while still hot.

2 To make the wonton dumplings: Parboil the spinach, drain, then put into a bowl of cold water for a couple of minutes to chill before draining again. Lightly squeeze the spinach to remove excess water, then chop.

3 In a bowl, add the minced pork, Chinese soup paste mix, sesame oil, soy sauce, shokoshu, and salt and pepper. Mix well with your hands. When it becomes sticky, add the spinach and chopped ginger and mix again.

4 Cut the wonton dumpling sheets in half and put a small teaspoon of the mix on each sheet. Fold the sheet diagonally across the mix. Seal the edges by using a little water on your finger, tracing a line around the inside edge of the pastry and then pressing the pastry together. Repeat with the rest of the wonton sheets and filling.

5 Reheat the stock, add the dumplings and simmer for 5–10 minutes. When they are cooked, add the soy sauce and shokoshu and season with salt and pepper. Finally, add the coriander and serve with chili oil.

Clear Soup with Julienne of Spring Vegetables

This is traditionally made with Japanese vegetables, such as udo, but you can substitute more readily available alternatives as suggested. Although I have used Chinese Soup paste here, you can also make it with dashi stock and get delicious results.

SERVES 4

^{1}/$_4$ lb. potatoes

^{1}/$_4$ cup carrots

^{1}/$_2$ cup udo, asparagus or celery

2^1/$_2$ tablespoons dried kikurage—optional

^{2}/$_3$ cup seri or flat-leaf parsley

3^1/$_3$ cups water

2 teaspoons Chinese soup paste

2 tablespoons sake

1 tablespoon potato starch or corn starch

salt

light soy sauce

chili powder or shichimi togarashi—to serve

1 Peel the potatoes and cut into julienne. Soak in water for 5–6 minutes to remove starch then pat dry. Peel the carrots and cut into thin julienne of 2–2^1/$_2$ inches. If using udo, peel, julienne and leave to soak in water for 5 minutes and pat dry. If using asparagus or celery, peel and julienne only.

2 Soak the dried kikurage in water until it softens, then rinse well. Discard the stalk and slice the rest finely. Cut the seri into 2- to 2^1/$_2$-inch lengths.

3 Pour the water, Chinese soup paste and sake into a pan and bring to a boil. Add the potatoes and carrots and simmer until just cooked.

4 Mix the potato starch with a little cold water and stir into the soup to thicken. Add the udo, kikurage and seri. Bring to a boil, season with salt and light soy sauce. Serve in soup bowls with chili powder or shichimi togarashi to taste.

Ingredients Note

Chinese soup paste tastes like a strong mixture of chicken and beef stock. If you cannot find it, this particular soup can be made with dashi stock instead; just use dashi in place of the water. In other cases you can substitute Chinese soup paste with a good-quality chicken stock mixed with a little beef stock.

Japanese-Style Mini Omelette

We Japanese are very good at adapting food from around the world to suit our taste. Japanese omelettes (omu rice) are often filled with cooked rice and topped with tomato sauce. Instead of tomato sauce, this recipe uses a sauce made with soy and dashi stock.

SERVES 2–4

1/2 cup cooked white crabmeat

2 shiitake mushrooms

3 wakegi, if available, or spring onions or chives

sunflower or vegetable oil, for frying

2 cups cooked rice

a little granulated chicken stock powder

1 teaspoon Harumi's All-Purpose Soy Sauce (see opposite)

salt and pepper

1–2 eggs

4 slivers of yuzu or lemon/lime zest—to garnish

For the sauce:

1/2 cup dashi stock or light fish stock

1/2 tablespoon mirin

1 teaspoon light soy sauce

pinch of salt

1 teaspoon potato starch or corn starch mixed with 1 teaspoon water

a little squeezed yuzu or lemon/lime juice

1 First make the filling. Roughly flake the crabmeat and check for any remaining pieces of shell. Remove and discard the stalks of the shiitake mushrooms, then cut the mushrooms into 1/2-inch square pieces and the wakegi into 1/2-inch lengths.

2 In a frying pan, heat 1 1/2 tablespoons of the sunflower oil. Add and stir-fry the ingredients in the following order: shiitake mushrooms, crabmeat, rice and the wakegi or spring onions. Finally add the granulated chicken stock powder, Harumi's All-Purpose Soy Sauce. Season with salt and pepper. Keep warm.

3 To make the sauce: In a small pan, combine the dashi stock, mirin, light soy sauce and salt and bring to a boil. Add the starch mixture to thicken and then add the yuzu juice.

4 Now beat the eggs in a bowl and season with salt and pepper. Heat 1/2–1 tablespoon of oil in a frying pan and add half the beaten egg mix to make a thin crepelike omelette. Divide the filling into two, place one portion on top of the omelette and fold in half. Repeat with the remaining eggs and filling. Cut each omelette in half and serve on a plate with the sauce poured over and garnished with yuzu zest.

Harumi's All-Purpose Soy Sauce
To make slightly more than 1²/₃ cups:
6-inch piece dried kombu seaweed
1²/₃ cups soy sauce
¹/₂ cup mirin
2 tablespoons superfine sugar
1 tablespoon dried fish flakes (katsuo bushi)

1 With a damp cloth, wipe the dried kombu to remove excess saltiness and then pat dry. Put the soy sauce and kombu in a small pan and leave to infuse for 30 minutes.

2 Place the pan on a low heat and add the mirin and sugar (making sure the sugar dissolves). Just before it comes to a boil, take out the kombu and skim the surface, if necessary. Bring to a boil, add the dried fish flakes, then turn off the heat when it comes back to a boil again. Leave to cool and strain. Pour into a sterilized bottle. This will keep in the fridge for about 2 weeks.

Sweet Egg Rolls

Tamago Yaki

We eat a lot of eggs in Japan, and this recipe is one of the most popular ways of eating them. I hope you will try it—it is easier than it first seems and is a useful technique to conquer; with it you can make many other types of egg rolls such as the ones we use for sushi. You can serve these egg rolls hot or cold in many different meals and they are also good in bento (lunch boxes).

MAKES 6 PIECES

¹/₄ cup mirin

4 eggs

4 tablespoons dashi stock or light fish stock

¹/₂ teaspoon light soy sauce

1 tablespoon superfine sugar

sunflower or vegetable oil

freshly grated daikon (mooli or Japanese
    white radish)

soy sauce—to taste

Harumi's Hint

If you do not have a rectangular frying pan try
using a small heavy-bottomed baking tray instead.

1   In a small heat-resistant bowl, add the mirin and microwave on medium uncovered for about 2 minutes and then leave to cool.

2   In a separate bowl, break the eggs and beat together. Then stir in the mirin and strain into a bowl. Dissolve the sugar in the dashi and soy sauce then add to the egg and mirin mixture.

3   Heat a little oil in a frying pan (we usually use a rectangular one—if you can find one, use it). Coat the pan with a little oil, using a piece of paper towel and chopsticks to remove any excess oil.

4   Pour in just enough of the egg mixture to coat the pan. As it sets, pull the cooked mixture toward the handle end of the pan, then roll it to the farthest end of the pan (see photos above). This will form the center (or core) of the roll.

5   Add a little more oil, if necessary. Then, lifting the already cooked egg roll, pour in some more of the egg mixture to make another thin layer.

6   When this layer sets, roll it toward you with the already cooked core in its center, then roll it again to the top of the pan. Repeat this several times building a thicker roll with each layer until you have used all of the mixture.

7   Remove the roll from the pan, wrap in wax paper, shape into a rectangular block and then leave for a short while to cool. Cut into thick slices (see photo left) and serve immediately with freshly grated daikon and soy sauce. If you are using the egg rolls in a bento (lunch box) make sure they are completely cool before putting into the box.

Tofu with Ricotta Cheese

You will be amazed at how well tofu and ricotta cheese go together, even though they are quite similar in taste and texture, and I think this sharp-sweet sauce provides the perfect balance to them both. Serve with plenty of cheese on top of the tofu and enjoy with a glass of chilled white wine.

SERVES 4

$1^1/_3$ cups soft/silken tofu
$^1/_4$ cup soy sauce
2 teaspoons superfine sugar
1 tablespoon mirin
$^1/_2$ tablespoon freshly grated ginger
$^1/_2$ cup ricotta cheese
5 shiso leaves or a mix of fresh basil and mint
dried fish flakes (katsuo bushi) and toasted sesame
   seeds—to garnish

1 Chill the tofu thoroughly before taking it out of the package, then drain it and place in a serving dish.

2 To make the sauce: Lightly mix the soy sauce, superfine sugar and mirin in a small, heat-resistant container. Microwave on medium for about 3 minutes without covering, then leave to stand for a few minutes before adding the freshly grated ginger.

3 Place the ricotta cheese on top of the tofu and sprinkle with the shredded shiso leaves, dried fish flakes and sesame seeds. Finally, pour over the warm sauce and serve immediately.

Eggplant Gratin with Tofu and Miso Sauce

We eat a great variety of gratins in Japan but this recipe using tofu and miso is not only lighter but also healthier than most and has a more Japanese flavor.
Serve with crusty French bread and a salad for a delicious lunch.

SERVES 4
1 eggplant
5 tablespoons sunflower or vegetable oil
1 teaspoon freshly grated garlic
salt and pepper
Tofu and Miso Sauce (see below)
3/4 cup grated parmesan cheese

1 Preheat the oven to 450°F.
2 Cut the eggplant into 1-inch-thick bite-size pieces and soak in water for about 5 minutes to remove any bitterness. Drain and pat dry.
3 Heat the oil in a frying pan on medium heat. Add the eggplant and brown both sides then season with the garlic, salt and pepper.
4 Pour half the Tofu and Miso Sauce into a large heat-resistant dish, cover with the cooked eggplant and sprinkle half of the cheese on top. Then pour over the remaining sauce and top with the remaining cheese. Put in the oven for about 20 minutes and cook until bubbling and lightly browned.

Tofu and Miso Sauce
This sauce is very easy to prepare in the microwave.

3/4 cup soft/silken tofu
2 tablespoons all-purpose flour
1 tablespoon cornstarch
3/4 cup milk (at room temperature)
1 tablespoon butter
1/2 teaspoon granulated chicken stock powder
1 tablespoon heavy cream
3 tablespoons red miso
3 tablespoons saikyo miso (see Harumi's Hint)
salt and coarsely ground black pepper

1 Drain the tofu, wrap in paper towels and place in a strainer for a few minutes to remove any excess water.
2 To make the sauce: Sift the flour and cornstarch into a heat-resistant bowl, gradually add the milk and mix together, taking care not to make it frothy. Cover the container and microwave on medium for 2 1/2 minutes. Mix thoroughly using a small whisk. Add the butter, granulated chicken stock powder and heavy cream and mix again.
3 While it is hot, add the red miso and saikyo miso and mix well.
4 Break up the tofu and blend into the sauce. Season with salt and pepper to taste.

Harumi's Hint
If you cannot find saikyo miso (a speciality miso from Kyoto—see page 123) please substitute both the red miso and saikyo miso with 5–6 tablespoons of awase miso and mix it with 2 tablespoons of superfine sugar.

Tofu with Edamame Beans and Chinese Pickles

Edamame beans are really popular in Japan, especially in summer when we eat them as an accompaniment to beer. They are almost nutty in flavor, particularly if you eat them out of their pods. It's not easy to find fresh ones outside Japan but you can buy them frozen. I like putting different textures and flavors together, and here the crunchiness of the beans and the saltiness of the pickles provides a wonderful balance to the soft tofu.

SERVES 4

1¹/₃ cups soft/silken tofu

1 tablespoon garlic oil (see page 64)

1 tablespoon chopped reconstituted shrimp (hoshi ebi) or boiled minced shrimp

1¹/₄ cups edamame beans, boiled and shelled

3 tablespoons chopped Chinese pickles (zaa sai), washed to remove any excess saltiness

1–2 teaspoons soy sauce

6 tablespoons roughly chopped peanuts

¹/₃ cup chopped spring onions or chives

Menu Planning

This dish would usually be served as a side dish and is especially good served in summer. I think it works well with any donburi dishes, Gyoza (page 70) or Pari Pari–Style Chicken (page 72).

1 Drain the tofu, wrap in paper towels and place in a strainer for a few minutes to drain off any excess water.

2 In a frying pan, heat the oil and when you can smell the garlic aroma, add the shrimp, edamame beans and Chinese pickles and cook quickly. Now add the soy sauce bit by bit, adjusting the amount according to how salty the Chinese pickles are.

3 Place the tofu in a serving dish, pour over the cooked mixture, then sprinkle over the peanuts and spring onions or chives and serve.

Tofu with Spicy Minced Topping

Mabo Dofu

This dish is loved by many people. If you are still a little nervous about tofu,
I recommend you try this recipe. I think you might be converted; the spicy mince
balances the smooth texture of the tofu so beautifully. It also has an appetizing
aroma from the many different ingredients: spring onion, garlic, ginger, sesame oil
and mizansho, all blended together to create a deep and complex flavor.

SERVES 4

2²/₃ cups soft/silken tofu

3/4 cup thinly sliced beef

a little soy sauce, pepper, sake and sesame oil

1 teaspoon Chinese soup paste mixed with
   ¹/₂ cup hot water

5 tablespoons soy sauce

2 teaspoons sugar

1 tablespoon sake

2 tablespoons sunflower or vegetable oil

2 cups spring onions, finely chopped

¹/₂ tablespoon finely chopped garlic

1 tablespoon finely chopped fresh ginger

¹/₂ tablespoon chili paste or to-ban-jan

1 tablespoon potato starch or corn flour mixed
   with 1 tablespoon water

salt and pepper

a little mizansho—see Ingredients Note

1 tablespoon sesame oil

1 Wrap the tofu in paper towels and leave in a strainer to remove
excess water.

2 Roughly cut up the beef and then leave to marinate in a mix
of a little soy sauce, pepper, sake and sesame oil—to taste. In a
separate cup or bowl, blend the Chinese soup paste mix, soy
sauce, sugar and sake and set aside.

3 In a frying pan, heat the oil and cook half the spring onions.
Add the garlic and ginger and continue cooking until a strong
aroma is released. Then add the chili paste and mix together.

4 Add the beef. When it turns brown, add the tofu, gently
breaking it up as you mix it in.

5 Add the Chinese soup, soy sauce, sugar and sake mix. When it
comes to a boil, stir in the potato starch mixture to thicken.
Season with salt and pepper and then sprinkle on the remaining
spring onions. Crush the mizansho, sprinkle over and finish with
a drizzle of sesame oil. Serve immediately.

Ingredients Note

Sansho is the name of a small citrus tree that
has buds called kinome and ripened fruit named
mizansho. Konazansho is the dried powder made
from the fruit. Its distinctive aroma is a great
addition to Japanese cooking. If you cannot find
mizansho you can substitute Szechuan pepper.

Menu Planning

This recipe is best served with white rice and a simple
vegetable dish, such as the bok choy recipe (page 115).

Rice & Noodles

Tuna and Avocado Small Donburi

Sometimes the simplest of recipes can be the tastiest. This donburi works well in so many ways; the colors, textures and mix of flavors are just wonderful. I always prepare this dish for my friends when I visit them overseas.

SERVES 4

1/4 lb. sashimi-quality raw tuna (chu toro—medium fatty tuna—is best for this recipe)
1/2 cup ripe avocado, peeled
3 3/4 cups hot cooked rice
1 tablespoon fresh ginger, finely chopped
soy sauce—to taste

What is a donburi?
A donburi is a large bowl, usually of hot rice, with a substantial topping to make it a satisfying meal, and is a common lunch dish. You can use all sorts of different foods for the topping.

Ingredients Note
Japanese rice is short grain and much stickier than long-grain rice. In general, you will need to cook around half a cup of rice per person.

1 With a sharp knife, roughly mince the tuna.
2 Cut the avocado into 1/2-inch square pieces and combine with the tuna.
3 Divide the hot rice among 4 bowls and put the tuna and avocado mix on top of each. Garnish with chopped ginger and add soy sauce to taste.

Peppers and Crab Mixed Rice

The red and green peppers make this rice dish very attractive. You can use it for any meal but its colors do seem to be rather festive! I use Japanese rice for this recipe but long-grain rice will also work.

SERVES 4–6
1¹/₂ cups uncooked rice
2 teaspoons granulated chicken stock powder or
   1 chicken bullion cube
1³/₄ cups water
¹/₂ cup red pepper
¹/₃ cup green pepper
5–6 mushrooms
¹/₂ cup cooked white crabmeat
1³/₄ tablespoons butter
1 bay leaf
salt and pepper

1 If using Japanese rice, wash, drain and leave to stand for 30 minutes before cooking.

2 Dissolve the chicken stock powder with a little hot water then add the remaining water.

3 Cut the peppers open and discard the seeds. Cut the red pepper into tiny square pieces (¹/₄ inch) and chop the green pepper into ¹/₂-inch square pieces. Slice the mushrooms thinly and loosen the crabmeat flakes, ensuring that there are no pieces of shell remaining. Cut the butter into small pieces.

4 Cook the rice (see page 54) in the chicken stock, adding the bay leaf for extra flavor.

5 Once the rice is cooked, stir in the butter, season with salt and pepper and roughly mix. Then add the peppers, mushrooms and crabmeat, mix again and serve.

Salmon Roe Rice with Salmon Flakes

This is a very useful recipe. You can serve the salmon flakes with ikura (salmon roe) on top of a bowl of rice or you can use just the salmon flakes to flavor rice balls for a bento (lunch box). The salmon keeps well in the fridge for 2–3 days and has a traditional flavor I think you will enjoy.

SERVES 2–4

For the salmon flakes:

1/2 lb. fillet fresh salmon, seasoned with salt and grilled until cooked

1 tablespoon sake

1 teaspoon light soy sauce

6 tablespoons furikake or toasted black sesame seeds

1 3/4 cups hot cooked rice

ikura (salmon roe)—to taste

chopped spring onions or chives—to garnish

Ingredients Note

Ikura is salted salmon roe and is very popular in Japan. We frequently use it in sushi or chirashi zushi. Furikake is a type of topping we sprinkle over rice, both hot and cold, and it usually includes toasted sesame seeds, bits of seaweed, dried fish and salt.

1 Discard any skin or bones on the salmon and flake the flesh.

2 Transfer the salmon to a small pan and pour over the sake. Put on a medium heat until cooked through. Flake again then add the light soy sauce.

3 Turn off heat and add the furikake or sesame seeds. You can either mix it in or just sprinkle on top, according to preference.

4 Put the cooked rice into individual bowls and put some of the salmon flakes on top. Add a spoonful of ikura and garnish with chopped spring onions or chives.

Rice with Green Peas

Green peas and rice are just a fantastic combination; tasty but also lovely to look at. Fresh spring green peas are the best to use, but out of season you can happily substitute frozen ones. This rice is good in a bento (lunch box). If you want a richer taste, add butter once cooked.

SERVES 4

1¹/₂ cups uncooked rice

1 tablespoon granulated chicken stock powder or
   1 chicken bullion cube

1³/₄ cups water

1 tablespoon sake

1 teaspoon light soy sauce

1¹/₂ cups fresh or frozen peas, cooked

salt

1 Wash the rice and leave to stand in a strainer for 30 minutes before cooking.

2 Mix the granulated chicken stock powder with a little hot water and then add more water to make 1³/₄ cups. Transfer the rice to a rice cooker or a saucepan, add the chicken stock, sake and light soy sauce, and cook as usual (see page 54).

3 Once cooked, lightly mix in the peas, taking care not to break up the rice or the peas. Season with a little salt and serve.

Menu Planning

This dish works really well with Ginger Pork (see page 62) but it's just as good with other meat dishes or fish.

Sea Bream Cooked on Rice

This fish is actually cooked twice, once under the grill then on top of the rice; it takes something tasty and makes it even tastier! Sea bream is often cooked on auspicious occasions, though usually we cook a whole fish. I think for this recipe though, a fillet is much easier. You can eat this as is or in a soup, ochazuke style (see below), and you can always substitute the sea bream with salmon.

SERVES 2

1 cup uncooked Japanese rice
1/4 lb. fresh sea bream fillet
salt
3/4 cup dashi stock or light fish stock
2/3 tablespoon light soy sauce
1/2 tablespoon mirin

To serve ochazuke style:
3/4 cup dashi stock or light fish stock
a little light soy sauce, sake and salt—to taste
chopped Japanese pickles—to taste

1 Wash and drain the rice then let stand for at least 30 minutes before cooking (see page 54).
2 Season the fillet of sea bream with salt then place under a hot grill until it turns a lovely golden color. Take off the heat and carefully remove any bones.
3 Place the rice, dashi stock, light soy sauce and mirin in a thick pan or earthenware pot that can take direct heat. Lightly mix and place the sea bream on top. Bring to a boil, then reduce the heat to low and cover. Cook for an additional 10 minutes. Remove from heat and leave to rest for 5–6 minutes. Take the skin off the fish, check for any remaining bones, mix in with the rice and serve.

To serve ochazuke style:

1 To make the soup: Heat the dashi stock, light soy sauce, sake and salt in a pan.
2 Spoon some of the sea bream and rice mixture into individual dishes and then pour over the hot soup. Garnish with chopped Japanese pickles, according to taste, and serve.

Sukiyaki Donburi

Along with sushi and sashimi, sukiyaki is one of the most well-known Japanese dishes. Usually we eat it "nabe style," in other words cooking it at the table in a casserole. However, here I am serving it as a donburi. It is also tasty served cold in a bento (lunch box).

SERVES 2

1 cup spring onions
2¼ tablespoons shungiku, if available, or arugula
1 cup shirataki noodles or thin rice noodles
1⅔ cups enoki mushrooms
¼ lb. thinly sliced beef
1½ tablespoons mirin
½ tablespoon superfine sugar
1 tablespoon sake
3 tablespoons Harumi's All-Purpose Soy Sauce
   (see page 33)
1¾ cups hot cooked rice
pickled ginger (beni shoga)—to taste

Ingredients Note

Shirataki are thin noodles of konnyaku, a jelly-like ingredient made from a vegetable root. Although it is rather tasteless it is added for its texture.

Shungiku leaves are part of the chrysanthemum family and have a strong, distinct flavor.

Enoki mushrooms are becoming more readily available around the world—they are thin and white and grow in clusters.

1 Cut the spring onions diagonally into ½-inch-thick pieces and then chop the shungiku into 1½-inch lengths.
2 Lightly cook the shirataki noodles and cut into short, easy-to-eat pieces.
3 Chop the bottom off the clump of enoki mushrooms and then cut the clump in half.
4 In a nonstick frying pan, lightly cook the beef and spring onions. Add the mirin, sugar, sake and Harumi's All-Purpose Soy Sauce. Then add the shirataki noodles and enoki mushrooms and simmer for a few minutes. Finally add the shungiku.
5 Serve the rice in bowls with the other cooked ingredients on top. Garnish with a little pickled ginger.

Minced Chicken Donburi

A chicken and egg donburi is a popular lunch dish where sweetened, simmered chicken is covered with a runny omelette. This is a lighter version of that tasty dish. It will serve two people as a main dish or four as a side dish. You can also use it cold in a bento (lunch box).

SERVES 2–4

For the chicken topping:

1 cup minced chicken
3 tablespoons soy sauce
1 tablespoon superfine sugar
1¹/₂ tablespoons mirin

For the sweetened shiitake mushrooms:

6 dried shiitake mushrooms, soaked in
  ¹/₄ cup water until soft
1¹/₂ tablespoons soy sauce
1¹/₂ tablespoons mirin
1 teaspoon superfine sugar

a few snow peas—to garnish
1 egg
3³/₄ cups hot cooked rice
nori seaweed—optional

1 To make the chicken topping: In a pan, mix the minced chicken, soy sauce, sugar and mirin together and simmer. Keep stirring until nearly all the liquid has evaporated.

2 To make the sweetened shiitake mushrooms: Soak the mushrooms in warm water until soft, then lightly squeeze to remove any excess water, reserving the water. Discard the mushroom stalks and slice each one into 6 pieces. Place in a small pan, add the reserved water, soy sauce, mirin and sugar, and simmer until most of the liquid has evaporated.

3 In a separate pan, parboil the snow peas, chill in cold water, drain and slice diagonally.

4 Boil the egg for 7–8 minutes then drain and place in a bowl of cold water for a couple of minutes so it will be cool enough to handle. Shell and chop the egg into 4 pieces.

5 Divide the rice into individual bowls. Serve the chicken with the shiitake mushrooms mixture on top, together with a few snow peas and the boiled egg. If using, crumble the nori over top according to taste.

Japanese Green Tea Risotto

Ochazuke

Every cuisine has its "nursery foods": comfort foods for when you are tired, foods that are perfect when you're not feeling well or don't have much of an appetite. Ochazuke is this dish in Japanese cuisine. It is an extremely simple dish to prepare and is very flexible—you can use many different ingredients, such as flaked salmon, as toppings. It is also a very popular way of ending an informal meal or an evening out.

a bowl of hot cooked Japanese rice per person
Japanese pickles (see page 126)
a pot of hot green tea

1 Place the hot cooked rice in a bowl, garnish with a selection of pickles and pour over the hot green tea. It couldn't be easier!

To cook Japanese rice
1 Wash the rice thoroughly by swishing it around in a bowl of cold water, draining and repeating the action a number of times. At first the water will be very cloudy but after washing for 3–4 minutes it will start to clear. Drain and leave for a minimum of 30 minutes before cooking.
2 If you do not have a rice cooker, use a heavy-bottomed saucepan with a tight-fitting lid. Put the rice in the pan and add water until there is slightly more water than rice. Do not salt.
3 Heat and just as the mixture comes to a boil put on the lid and turn the heat down low. Simmer for 15 minutes then switch off the heat and leave covered for an additional 10 minutes before serving.

Chilled Noodles with Pork

These chilled noodles with sesame dressing make a refreshing lunch on a hot summer's day.

SERVES 4

1 lb. boneless pork loin joint
1 teaspoon soy sauce
1/2 tablespoon shokoshu or dry sherry
1 teaspoon sesame oil
a little salt
2/3 cup cucumber
1 cup spring onions
sunflower or vegetable oil—for deep frying
a little potato starch or corn flour—for dusting
1 1/3 lbs. ready-to-cook Chinese egg noodles
coarsely ground toasted sesame seeds—to garnish
mustard—optional

For the sesame dressing:

1/4 cup soy sauce
1 tablespoon superfine sugar
1 tablespoon rice vinegar
1 tablespoon sesame paste or unsweetened smooth peanut butter
a little granulated chicken stock powder mixed with 2 tablespoons hot water

1 Cut the pork into 8 slices and lightly score each slice on both sides; this helps it cook quickly. Marinate in the soy sauce, shokoshu, sesame oil and a little salt.

2 Slice the cucumber diagonally and then chop each piece into thin strips, discarding the watery center. Chop the spring onions in half lengthways, slice diagonally into thin julienne and then soak in water to take away any sharpness.

3 To make the dressing: Mix together the soy sauce, superfine sugar, rice vinegar, sesame paste and chicken stock.

4 Heat the oil in a pan. Dust the pork with potato starch and deep-fry until cooked through.

5 Cook the noodles, following the instructions on the package. Plunge into icy water to cool and then drain.

6 Divide the noodles among four bowls. Arrange the pork on top, garnish with the cucumber and spring onions and pour over the sauce. Sprinkle sesame seeds on top. Serve with mustard, to taste.

Harumi's Soba Chirashi

I love putting a variety of ingredients on top of cooked soba noodles to create fun and interesting dishes. For this particular recipe I like to use sweet egg rolls, vegetable tempura, kamaboko, shiso leaves, nori seaweed and a variety of toppings. I normally serve this for lunch but it is also ideal for parties; just line up all the ingredients on a table and your guests can add whatever they like.

SERVES 2

For 1¹/₂ cups mentsuyu sauce:
¹/₂ cup soy sauce
¹/₂ cup mirin
³/₄ cup water
2 tablespoons dried fish flakes (katsuo bushi)

1²/₃ cups soba noodles
sweet egg roll pieces (see page 34)
sliced kamaboko—optional (see Ingredients Note)
vegetable tempura pieces (see page 112)

Optional toppings:
grated daikon (mooli or Japanese white radish)
freshly grated ginger
chili powder or shichimi togarashi
toasted white sesame seeds
roughly chopped mitsuba or coriander
grated wasabi
chopped spring onions or chives

Ingredients Note
Kamaboko is a mild-flavored fish paste loaf, semi-cylindrical in shape. To serve, it is sliced and sometimes eaten with soy sauce.

If you cannot find dried fish flakes, substitute half the water with ¹/₂ cup of light fish stock. It should not have a strong fishy flavor, just a slight tang.

1 To make the mentsuyu: Put the soy sauce, mirin, water and dried fish flakes in a heat-resistant bowl and lightly mix. Microwave on medium uncovered for about 3¹/₂ minutes. Leave to cool for a few minutes then pour into a jug to serve.

2 Cook the soba noodles, following the instructions on the packet. When done, rinse under cold running water and drain well.

3 Place all the toppings on serving dishes on the table. Divide the soba noodles into bowls. Serve pieces of sweet egg roll, kamaboko and tempura on top of the noodles. Choose toppings to taste and pour a little mentsuyu sauce over top.

Homemade Udon

Most people these days buy ready-made fresh or dried udon noodles but if you cannot find them easily you can always make them. It doesn't matter how uneven the noodles are. They are fun to make and have a great texture.

SERVES 4
1 cup water
5 teaspoons salt
3½ cups bread flour
1½ cups all-purpose flour
bread flour—for dusting

For the Hot Udon
Serves 1

1²/₃–2 cups homemade udon noodles
1 cup dashi stock
⅓ cup Basic Mentsuyu Sauce (see opposite)
finely chopped spring onions—to taste
chili powder or shichimi togarashi—to taste

1 Take a tablespoon of the water and mix with the salt. Once it has dissolved, add to the remaining water. Then, in a large bowl, combine the flours before adding the salted water.

2 Using your hands, mix the flour and water to make a dough. Pull the dough up from the bottom of the bowl and press down. Repeat until well combined.

3 Take the dough out of the bowl and knead it on a board as hard as you can for 5–10 minutes. Transfer it to a big plastic bag and wrap it in a thick towel. Put it on the floor, take your shoes off and walk on it (see photo opposite)—this helps to give the final noodles a good chewy texture.

4 Remove the flattened dough from the bag and roll it out. Then fold it up, put it back in the bag and walk on it again. Repeat this a number of times over a 15- to 20-minute period, until the dough becomes really smooth. Then leave the dough, still in the bag, for 3–4 hours. In winter, leave it in a warm place.

5 Take the dough out of the bag, shape it into a ball again, then return it to the bag and walk on it. Try to spread the dough with your feet—try turning 360 degrees on your heels—it helps to spread the dough quite efficiently.

6 Dust your work surface with flour, place the flattened dough on top and roll out from the middle. Rotate the dough and continue rolling until it is ⅛-inch thick and roughly square in shape.

7 Dust the work surface and the dough again then fold into three, accordion style (the folded dough should be around 4 inches in width).

8 Slice the dough into ⅛-inch-width lengths. You will find this easier if you use a large wide knife not just to cut but also to push the noodle strips away from the remaining dough. The dough gets very sticky so keep dusting with flour as you cut.

9 Fill a large saucepan with plenty of water and bring to a boil. Dust the noodles with flour again, if necessary, before adding to the boiling water.

10 Using cooking chopsticks (saibashi), lightly stir the noodles to prevent them from sticking together.

11 As the water boils, add a small cupful of cold water to reduce the temperature. Repeat this when necessary and continue to cook for 6–7 minutes. Once cooked, drain the noodles in a sieve and rinse under cold running water so they cool rapidly.

12 Once cool enough to handle, separate out the noodles with your hands and carry on rinsing to ensure all the starch is removed.

13 The udon are now ready. You can serve them cold but they are more traditionally served hot, as below.

Hot Udon

1 Place the udon in a sieve or a colander. Bring a kettleful of water to a boil and pour it over the noodles to heat them, then drain well and place in individual bowls. Mix three parts dashi stock (see page 20) with one part Mentsuyu Sauce and heat in a pan. As it comes to a boil, turn the heat off and pour over the udon. Sprinkle with chopped spring onions and chili powder or shichimi togarashi to taste.

Basic Mentsuyu Sauce

1 Lightly wipe the dried kombu seaweed to remove any excess saltiness. Put into a pan with the water and soak for 2–3 hours.

2 Add the soy sauce, mirin and sugar and heat. Just before it comes to a boil, remove the kombu seaweed and add the dried fish flakes.

3 Boil for about 30 seconds then turn off the heat. Cool and strain.

4 Pour into a sterilized bottle. You can keep this refrigerated for up to 3–4 days.

For the Basic Mentsuyu Sauce
SERVES 4
4-inch piece dried kombu seaweed
1 cup water
1¾ cups soy sauce
1¼ cups mirin
2 tablespoons superfine sugar
4½ tablespoons dried fish flakes (katsuo bushi)

Meat & Poultry

Ginger Pork
Buta no Shoga Yaki

As a young wife, I quickly realized that my husband loved to eat this dish together with Rice with Green Peas (see page 48). I have served up this combination so many times you would think that my family would be tired of it, but it seems to be just as popular as ever and is enjoyed by all of us.

SERVES 4
3 1/2 cups bean sprouts
3 tablespoons soy sauce
2 tablespoons mirin
1/2–1 tablespoon freshly grated ginger—to taste
2/3 lb. finely sliced pork
sunflower or vegetable oil, for stir-frying the pork
1 tablespoon sunflower or vegetable oil, for cooking the bean sprouts
3/4 tablespoon sliced garlic (1 clove)
salt and pepper

1 Trim the ends off the bean sprouts. (Yes, I know you might think that this is not worth doing but try it once and I think you will agree that bean sprouts not only look nicer but they also taste better if they have been trimmed. Try it!)
2 Mix together the soy sauce, mirin and grated ginger and dip the pork into this marinade briefly just before cooking.
3 Heat a little oil in a frying pan over medium heat. Remove the pork from the marinade and add to the pan, making sure it cooks evenly and doesn't stick together or curl up. Turn over after a couple of minutes and cook until both sides are browned. Don't leave the pork for long, as it cooks surprisingly quickly, but make sure it's cooked through.
4 In a separate frying pan, heat a tablespoon of oil over a high heat. Add the sliced garlic. When the aroma is released, add the bean sprouts and stir-fry. Season with salt and pepper.
5 Put the bean sprouts onto a serving dish and then lay the slices of pork on top. Pour any remaining juices from the frying pan over the pork.

Ginger Pork Salad

Buta no Shoga Yaki Salad

This is a variation on the previous Ginger Pork recipe. It is a useful dish to serve for lunch or as a light supper. You can serve it with crusty French bread or a bowl of hot white rice.

SERVES 4

For the Ginger Pork:
1/2 tablespoon freshly grated ginger
2 tablespoons soy sauce
1 teaspoon mirin
1/2 lb. finely sliced pork
mixed salad leaves
sunflower or vegetable oil

For the dressing:
1 tablespoon freshly grated ginger
1 tablespoon wine vinegar
4 tablespoons soy sauce
2 tablespoons sunflower or vegetable oil
2 teaspoons superfine sugar
pepper

Harumi's Hint
I always use pork shoulder or loin for this dish, as it has a good amount of fat, making the meat tender. The thickness of the pork slices depends on your preference. You should also ensure that the pork is at room temperature when you are ready to cook.

1 To make the Ginger Pork: Mix the grated ginger, soy sauce and mirin together and briefly marinate the pork. Soak the salad leaves in cold water with ice cubes to make them crispy, then drain well.
2 To make the dressing: Mix together the grated ginger, wine vinegar, soy sauce, oil, sugar and pepper.
3 Heat a little oil in a frying pan and cook the pork on both sides. Make sure the slices don't overlap so they brown evenly.
4 Arrange the salad leaves in a dish and place the pork on top. Pour the dressing over and serve.

Pork with Aromatic Vegetables

This is a very simple but extremely tasty dish. The aroma from the toppings is simply wonderful. It is also a really useful recipe for when you are in a hurry.

SERVES 4

1/2 lb. finely sliced pork
salt and pepper
2/3 cup mitsuba or coriander
1 cup spring onions
1 1/2 tablespoons fresh ginger, peeled
2 myoga (if available)
10 shiso leaves or a mix of fresh mint and basil
a little garlic oil (see method below)
toasted sesame seeds—to garnish
a mix of soy sauce and wasabi—to taste—or
 sudachi or lemon/lime juice—to taste

1 Season the pork with salt and pepper.
2 Chop up the mitsuba into bite-size pieces. Finely chop the spring onions, then cut the ginger, myoga and shiso leaves into strips.
3 Heat the garlic oil in a frying pan and stir-fry the pork until crisp. Place in a serving dish.
4 Cover generously with the mitsuba, spring onions, ginger, shiso and myoga and then sprinkle toasted sesame seeds on top. Pour over the soy sauce and wasabi mix or the squeezed sudachi juice to taste.

To make garlic oil:

1 Finely chop 3 cloves of fresh garlic and add to 3/4 cup sunflower or vegetable oil. This will keep in the fridge for up to 1 week. It is useful for dressings, stir-fries and pasta.

Menu Planning
Serve this with white rice, miso shiru and a vegetable side dish such as Sautéed Bean Sprouts with Bok Choy (see page 115).

Pork in Crispy Breadcrumbs

Tonkatsu

Tonkatsu is a classic Japanese dish that is just delicious. The outside should be crispy, while the pork inside remains succulent. It is always served next to a mountain of finely shredded cabbage and often has tonkatsu sauce drizzled on top just before serving. I like using a combination of salt, lemon and mustard as an alternative to this sauce.

1 Make 4–5 cuts through the fat into the pork loin to prevent the meat from curling up while cooking.

2 Tenderize the pork with a mallet or rolling pin, then season with salt and pepper.

3 Dust the pork pieces with flour then dip into the beaten egg and finally into the breadcrumbs.

4 Heat the oil to 320–340°F and deep-fry the pork for 2–3 minutes, turn once then continue cooking for another 2–3 minutes until cooked through.

5 When golden, remove from the oil and drain well. Slice each loin into bite-size pieces and place next to a pile of finely shredded cabbage. Serve with a choice of tonkatsu sauce, lemon, salt and soy sauce.

SERVES 4
1 lb. thick-cut pork loins (¹/₃- to ²/₃-inch thick)
salt and pepper
all-purpose flour—for dusting
1 egg, beaten
breadcrumbs as needed
sunflower or vegetable oil—for deep frying
shredded cabbage and tonkatsu sauce, lemon, salt,
    soy sauce—to taste

Harumi's Hint

You can judge the temperature of the oil by dropping in a few breadcrumbs. If they sink to the bottom of the pan before coming back to the surface, the temperature is low. If they sink to the middle of the pan and return to the surface, the temperature is medium. If they don't sink but just move around on the surface, then it is hot. A medium temperature is best for cooking tonkatsu. If the pork is fresh you can freeze the prepared tonkatsu pork pieces after coating with the breadcrumbs, wrapping in plastic wrap and putting them in the freezer. Defrost thoroughly before deep-frying.

Mini Tonkatsu

Bite-size pieces of tonkatsu are easy to make and fun to eat—great for parties or bento (lunch boxes).

1   Cut the pork into 3/4- to 1¼-inch square pieces. Chop some baby leeks into 3/4- to 1¼-inch pieces. Dust with flour and then coat the pork and leeks separately in beaten egg and breadcrumbs. Deep-fry at 320–340°F until crispy. Thread the pork and leeks onto skewers and serve accompanied by ponzu sauce, sudachi and salt.

Chicken Kebabs

Yakitori

I think most people have heard of yakitori, Japanese grilled chicken kebabs. There are many recipes for making them, but here are the two classics. You can grill them in your kitchen or cook them on a barbecue. Most specialist yakitori restaurants use charcoal to give an extra-smoky flavor to the chicken.

SERVES 4

2¹/₃ cups baby leeks or spring onions
¹/₄ lb. boneless chicken thighs with skin on
8 chicken wings
¹/₂ lb. chicken gizzards or livers
salt and pepper
lemon and mustard—to serve

Simple Yakitori Kebabs

This is the easiest version of yakitori. The kebabs are simply seasoned with salt and pepper. You can use any parts of the chicken for this but try to have a good variety. In the photo above, you can see simple yakitori made with chicken wings, chicken gizzards and chicken thighs with baby leeks. If you have problems finding gizzards, or don't like them, then try something like chicken livers instead.

Harumi's Hint

If you are using wooden skewers, wrap foil around the ends to prevent them from burning and to make them easier to handle.

SERVES 4

For the Sweet Yakitori Sauce:

1/2 cup mirin

3 tablespoons sake

1/2 cup soy sauce

1/4 cup superfine sugar

For the Minced Chicken Yakitori (Tsukune):

2/3 lb. minced chicken

1/2 cup onion, finely minced

2 tablespoons sake

1 tablespoon all-purpose flour

salt

a little superfine sugar

ao-nori seaweed—to garnish

1 Cut the baby leeks into 1-inch-length pieces and cut the chicken thighs into bite-size pieces. Thread them onto the skewers, alternating the leeks and chicken.

2 Cut the chicken wings in half lengthways and skewer with 2 or 3 skewers (see photo). (If the chicken wings still have tips—i.e., rather meatless, pointed ends to the wings—then remove them before preparing.)

3 Prepare the gizzards or liver, cutting into bite-size pieces, and thread onto small skewers.

4 Season the prepared skewers with salt and pepper and cook on a medium heat, either on a charcoal barbecue or under a grill. When cooked, serve immediately with wedges of lemon and some mustard.

Sweet Yakitori Sauce:

This lightly sweetened sauce is another very popular way of cooking yakitori, especially for children. The sauce can be used on the Simple Yakitori Kebabs but I think it works equally well with Minced Chicken Yakitori (Tsukune).

1 To make the sauce: In a small pan, mix together the mirin, sake, soy sauce and sugar and simmer over a medium heat until it starts to thicken. Set aside until ready to use.

2 To make the minced chicken yakitori: Preheat the oven to 400°F. Line a baking tray with foil or wax paper. In a bowl, mix all the ingredients except the ao-nori with your hands. Divide and shape the mixture into 8 sausage-shaped kebabs. Put on the baking tray and cook in the oven for 10 minutes. When cooked, thread them onto skewers, brush with the sauce and either grill or barbecue. Serve with ao-nori sprinkled over top.

Ingredients Note

Ao-nori is a finely chopped seaweed often used as a garnish on top of cooked foods, such as okonomiyaki (a thick Japanese savory pancake).

Chinese-Style Dumplings

Gyoza

There are many recipes for gyoza. At the moment, this is my favorite. For the best results you need to have patience when preparing the ingredients. The ginger, garlic and spring onions must be chopped as finely as possible to ensure they blend together. I also use plenty of nira (see Ingredients Note) in this recipe and recommend that you take the time to cut each strand of nira in half lengthways before finely chopping; it might seem unnecessarily fiddly but it does give the mixture a better texture. It's worth using potato starch as it helps make these dumplings crispy. Gyoza are a wonderful addition to any party but you can also have them as a side dish.

MAKES 48 DUMPLINGS

⅓ cup cabbage
⅓ cup Chinese cabbage
½ teaspoon salt
2 cups nira (garlic chives) or spring onions and garlic
½ cup minced pork
2 tablespoons lard (at room temperature)
½ cup hot water mixed with 1 teaspoon Chinese soup paste or rich chicken stock
1 tablespoon sesame oil
1 tablespoon shokoshu or dry sherry
1½ tablespoons (2 cloves) fresh garlic, finely chopped
1 tablespoon fresh ginger, finely chopped
1 cup spring onions, finely chopped
salt and pepper
48 thin round pastry skins (you can find these in most Chinese supermarkets)
potato starch or corn starch—as needed
sunflower or vegetable oil

For the dipping sauce:

Soy sauce, rice vinegar with a few drops of chili oil (la-yu)—to taste

1 Finely chop the two types of cabbage. Mix them together in a bowl, season with salt and set aside to use later. Cut the nira in half lengthways and finely chop.

2 In a separate bowl, combine the pork and lard by hand. Add the Chinese soup mix, leave to cool, then add the sesame oil, shokoshu, finely chopped garlic, ginger and spring onions. Mix together before adding the nira.

3 Squeeze the cabbage to remove excess water. Add to the meat

Ingredients Note

Nira is a pungent green herb of the onion family that looks like a thick chive and smells strongly of garlic. If you can't find nira, finely chop some spring onions or chives together with 1 large clove of garlic and mix together.

Deep-Fried Dumplings (makes 24)

This is a variation on gyoza using the same recipe in a slightly different way. Place a spoonful of stuffing on a pastry skin and wet the edge with water. Cover with another pastry skin and, first making sure that there is no air inside, use a fork to seal the edges. In a frying pan, heat enough oil to deep fry. Cook until both sides are crispy. Serve with dipping sauce.

mixture, season with salt and pepper and stir to combine.

4 The stuffing is now ready, and you can either use it now or refrigerate overnight and use the next day.

5 Place an even spoonful of stuffing onto each pastry skin. Wet the edges of the skin with water and pleat them to seal, as shown above.

6 Dust each dumpling with a little potato starch. Heat a small quantity of oil in a large frying pan. Shake the dumplings to remove any excess potato starch and then arrange them in rows in the pan.

7 Add enough water to come a third of the way up the dumplings, cover and cook over a medium heat until the water has evaporated and you can see the bottoms of the dumplings changing color.

8 Remove the lid and drizzle a little oil over the dumplings. Cook uncovered, until the bottoms are crispy, then turn them over to brown both sides. Place on a large serving dish

9 To make the dipping sauce: Mix together soy sauce, rice vinegar and a few drops of la-yu. Eat with the hot dumplings.

Pari Pari–Style Chicken

This is a wonderful, easy dish to prepare, especially as the oven does most of the work. To make the chicken nice and crispy you need to brush the skin with sesame oil halfway through cooking. You can enjoy the chicken as it is but you might also want to try it with Worcestershire sauce. It is best served with a bowl of rice and some tasty vegetables. You can serve it as a side or main dish, though you might want to increase the amounts if you serve it as a main dish for 4 people.

SERVES 4

1¹/₂ lbs. chicken thighs on the bone with skin on
1 tablespoon shokoshu or dry sherry
1 tablespoon soy sauce
¹/₂ tablespoon sesame oil
1 teaspoon freshly grated garlic
pepper
2 tablespoons sesame oil—to coat the chicken
Worcestershire sauce—optional

1 De-bone the chicken. Lightly score the chicken skin.
2 Mix together the shokoshu, soy sauce, sesame oil, garlic and pepper and marinate the chicken for about 15 minutes.
3 Preheat the oven to 425°F. Cover a baking tray with foil and place the chicken on it, skin side up. Bake for 20 minutes, then remove and brush with sesame oil. Continue cooking for about 10 minutes more until the skin is crispy.
4 Remove from the oven. While hot, cut the chicken into smaller pieces and arrange on a serving plate. Serve with Worcestershire sauce, if desired.

Menu Planning
This works particularly well with Peppers and Crab Mixed Rice (see page 46), Clear Soup with Pork and Spinach Wonton Dumplings (see page 28) and Baked Papaya with Coconut Milk (see page 134).

Chicken and Green Bean Salad

Cooking chicken with sake, ginger and spring onions gives it a subtle and interesting flavor. This is good for a summer party or to serve as a side dish for a special dinner.

SERVES 4
½ lb. chicken breast
green part of a spring onion
2 teaspoons ginger, crushed
1 tablespoon sake
1⅓ cups green beans
3 tablespoons mayonnaise
1 tablespoon milk
1 teaspoon granulated chicken stock powder
salt and pepper

1 To measure the amount of water needed, put the chicken breast into a small pan and add just enough cold water to cover, then remove the chicken and bring the water to a boil. Return the chicken to the pan with the spring onion, ginger and sake. Simmer until the chicken is cooked. Remove and leave to cool.
2 String the beans and chop in half diagonally. Parboil for a few minutes, taking care not to overcook them. Drain and pat dry.
3 Roughly shred the chicken when it is cool enough to handle.
4 Place the beans and chicken in a bowl. Combine the mayonnaise, milk and granulated chicken stock powder and stir into the beans and chicken. Season with salt and pepper and serve.

Chicken with Soy and Balsamic Dressing

This is an unusual combination of flavors but I think it works really well. It is also a very quick recipe to make, and many of the ingredients you will probably already have at home. I think this is a perfect mid-week meal.

SERVES 4
2 tablespoons soy sauce
1 tablespoon balsamic vinegar
1 clove garlic, sliced
coarsely ground black pepper
1 lb. boneless chicken thighs with skin on
a little sunflower or vegetable oil
a few basil leaves—to garnish

For the sautéed cabbage:
$1/2$–$3/4$ cup cabbage
1 tablespoon sunflower or vegetable oil
1 tablespoon butter
salt and pepper

1 Put the soy sauce, balsamic vinegar, garlic and pepper in a bowl and stir to combine. Cut the chicken diagonally into bite-size pieces and marinate in the mixture for about 30 minutes.
2 Heat the oil in a frying pan and fry the chicken, turning halfway to brown both sides.
3 To make the sautéed cabbage: Roughly chop the cabbage into large pieces. In a wok or frying pan, heat the oil and butter, add the cabbage, sauté until cooked, then lightly season with salt and pepper.
4 Place the cabbage on a serving dish and arrange the chicken on top. Pour over any remaining sauce from the chicken pan and garnish with basil leaves.

Easy meal + sauce ✓ +

Teriyaki Hamburgers

I like using raw onions in these hamburgers. It gives an extra bite and makes them much tastier. In Japan we love hamburgers cooked this way, with teriyaki sauce poured over and served with rice and vegetables. These hamburgers are great for bento, too. You can substitute the teriyaki sauce for ponzu soy sauce for a different flavor. Teriyaki sauce can be used for almost any food but it's particularly good with meat and fish.

MAKES 8 HAMBURGERS
2½ tablespoons breadcrumbs
½ cup milk
⅔ lb. minced beef
⅓ lb. minced pork
1⅓ cups onions, roughly chopped
1 egg
½ teaspoon salt
pepper
½ tablespoon butter
4–5 tablespoons teriyaki sauce

For the teriyaki sauce:
1 cup mirin
½ cup soy sauce
1½–2 tablespoons superfine sugar

Harumi's Hint

It is better to use the oven for larger hamburgers like these. Brown the outsides in a frying pan and then put in the oven until cooked. It is a foolproof method. While the hamburgers are in the oven, you can prepare the vegetables. However, if you are making smaller hamburgers for bento (lunch boxes), you can simply cook in a frying pan and you don't need to use the oven. In this case, pour the teriyaki sauce over the hamburgers in the frying pan once they are cooked.

1 Place the breadcrumbs in a small bowl and add the milk. Set aside until all the liquid is absorbed. In a large bowl, combine the beef, pork, chopped onions, soaked breadcrumbs and egg. Season with salt and pepper and, using your hands, mix well until sticky. Divide the mixture and shape into hamburgers, patting lightly on both sides to make them really firm.

2 Preheat the oven to 450°F. Over medium heat, melt the butter in a frying pan or skillet that can go into the oven. Brown the hamburgers on both sides then put them into the oven and cook for another 15 minutes.

3 To make the teriyaki sauce: In a small pan, heat the mirin over low heat for 1–2 minutes then add the soy sauce and sugar and simmer for an additional 1–2 minutes.

4 Pour the teriyaki sauce over the cooked burgers and serve on a bed of vegetables.

Menu Planning

I like to serve these hamburgers on a bed of simply cooked vegetables. In the photo opposite, I have used 1 cup potatoes, $\frac{1}{2}$ cup carrots, 10 green beans and 1 cup broccoli. Peel the potatoes and cut into bite-size pieces. Soak in cold water and drain. Line a microwave suitable dish with paper towels, put the potato on top and cover with plastic wrap. Microwave for $2\frac{1}{2}$ minutes until just cooked through. Parboil the carrots, green beans and broccoli separately, and then sauté them and the potatoes in 1 tablespoon of oil. Season with a little salt and pepper and serve them nicely crisp.

Chicken Rolled in Sesame Seeds

You can also use small pieces of boneless chicken thighs or chicken breasts for this recipe. The chicken pieces can be eaten hot or cold and are a useful addition to a bento (lunch box).

SERVES 4

8 chicken wings with skin on
1/2 tablespoon soy sauce
1/2 tablespoon shokoshu or dry sherry
sunflower or vegetable oil, for deep frying
white and black toasted sesame seeds
lime wedges——to serve

For the sauce:

1/4 cup soy sauce
3 tablespoons superfine sugar
2 tablespoons shokoshu or dry sherry
1 star anise

1 Rinse the chicken pieces and pat dry. Chop off any wing tips at the first joint (you can use them to make stock—see page 20). Prick the chicken pieces with a fork and marinate in the soy sauce and shokoshu for about 10 minutes.

2 To make the sauce: In a small saucepan, heat the soy sauce, sugar, shokoshu and star anise until the mixture starts to thicken.

3 Remove the chicken from the marinade and pat dry. Heat the oil in a wok or deep frying pan. Add the chicken and cook at a low temperature until almost cooked, then turn up the heat and cook until crispy.

4 Remove the hot chicken pieces from the oil and dip one side only into the sauce (see Harumi's Hint, below). Quickly place the dipped side down into the toasted sesame seeds and press hard to coat. Serve with wedges of lime.

Harumi's Hint

This sauce is quite rich, so you can choose whether to coat each piece of chicken or just one side.

Teriyaki Chicken

You can buy bottles of ready-made teriyaki sauce but when it is so easy to prepare, why not make it yourself? It is a very versatile sauce for cooking pork, beef, salmon or mackerel. This dish is popular with everyone and can be served both hot and cold.

SERVES 4
1¹/₄ lbs. chicken breasts with skin on
salt and pepper
¹/₂ tablespoon sunflower or vegetable oil
2–3 tablespoons Teriyaki Sauce (see page 76)
mixed salad—to serve
a little mustard—to serve

1 Lightly season the chicken with salt and pepper. Heat the oil in a frying pan on medium heat, brown both sides of the chicken and leave until cooked through.
2 Add the Teriyaki Sauce and continue to cook until it has glazed and covered the chicken. Remove the pan from the heat, slice and serve the chicken with a crispy mixed salad and mustard. Pour any remaining sauce from the frying pan over chicken.

Harumi's Hint
To make salad leaves nice and crispy, leave them in very cold water for a short while before draining and patting dry with paper towels. If you make sure the leaves are completely dry and then put them in an airtight bag in the fridge, they will stay fresh and crisp for a day or so.

Quick-Fried Steak with Two Types of Japanese Dressing

If you have read my first book you will know that I love steak. This is a great way to serve it with two different dressings, each of which has a distinctive Japanese flavor.

SERVES 4

For the citrus soy sauce:
(this needs to be prepared the day before)
½ cup Harumi's All-Purpose Soy Sauce (see page 33)
1 teaspoon Chinese pepper
1 sudachi or lemon/lime sliced

For the shiso mayonnaise:
¼ cup mayonnaise
2 tablespoons milk
a little granulated chicken stock powder, pepper and light soy sauce
20 shiso leaves or a mix of fresh mint and basil, roughly chopped

For the creamy mashed potatoes:
1²/₃ cup potatoes
1 tablespoon butter
1 cup heavy cream
a little salt, pepper and granulated chicken stock powder

For the steaks:
2 sirloin beef steaks, 1 inch thick
salt and pepper
1 teaspoon freshly grated garlic
a little sunflower or vegetable oil
wasabi—to taste
sudachi—to taste

1   To make the citrus soy sauce: Mix together Harumi's All-Purpose Soy Sauce, Chinese pepper and sudachi in a small bowl and leave overnight.

2   To make the shiso mayonnaise: In a small bowl, combine the mayonnaise, milk, granulated chicken stock powder, pepper and light soy sauce. Just before serving, stir in the chopped shiso leaves.

3   To make the mashed potatoes: Peel the potatoes, cut into bite-size pieces and soak in water for 5–6 minutes to remove any excess starch. Drain and place on paper towels in a heat-resistant container. Cover and microwave on medium for about 5 minutes until cooked.

4   Place the potatoes in a bowl and mash while still hot. Add the butter and heavy cream and mash again. Season with salt, pepper and the granulated chicken stock powder.

5   Season the beef with salt and pepper. Rub in the grated garlic. In a frying pan, heat a little oil over a high heat. Add the steaks, browning each side, and cook to your personal preference.

6   Chop the steaks into bite-size pieces and either place on one large serving dish or individual plates. Serve with the mashed potatoes, the two types of sauce and wasabi and sudachi to taste.

Harumi's Hint
The steaks should be at room temperature before you cook them. This makes it easier to accurately gauge the cooking time. I also recommend you cook both sides of the steak on a very high heat.

Fried Chicken with Spring Onion Sauce

My family loves this dish and when I introduced it to my readers, they loved it too! It is a very useful dish for parties. Use plenty of potato starch to coat the chicken, take your time when you deep-fry and you will have good results every time. The spicy spring onion sauce goes really well with the fried chicken.

SERVES 4

1¼ lbs. boneless chicken thighs with skin on
1 tablespoon soy sauce
1 tablespoon shokoshu or dry sherry
pepper
potato starch or corn starch, for coating the chicken
sunflower or vegetable oil—for deep frying
iceburg lettuce, roughly chopped—to serve

For the spring onion sauce:

½ tablespoon sunflower or vegetable oil
1 cup spring onions, roughly chopped
1 dried red chili or ½ a large fresh chili, chopped
½ cup soy sauce
1 tablespoon shokoshu or dry sherry
1 tablespoon rice vinegar
1½ tablespoons superfine sugar

1 Prick the chicken skin with a fork. Mix the soy sauce, shokoshu and pepper in a bowl, add the chicken and marinate for 10–15 minutes. When you are ready to cook, drain well and then coat each piece with plenty of potato starch.

2 Heat the oil to 340°F and deep-fry the chicken until it is crispy and cooked all the way through. Do not put too many chicken pieces in at once, as it lowers the temperature of the oil. Drain well on paper towels and cut into finger-size pieces.

3 To make the spring onion sauce: Heat the oil in a frying pan over medium heat. Quickly stir-fry the spring onions and chopped chili, add the soy sauce, shokoshu, rice vinegar and sugar, and immediately turn off the heat.

4 Soak the lettuce in cold water to make it crispy, pat dry and place on a serving dish. Arrange the chicken on top and pour the spring onion sauce over chicken. Serve immediately.

Harumi's Hint

After removing any excess oil from cooked chicken, let it rest a short while before cutting it into pieces. The chicken will continue to cook a little more and retain its juices, so you will still have to be careful not to burn your fingers when you cut it up.

Meat and Potato Stew

Nikujaga

This delicious traditional stew has a slightly sweet and salty flavor. It's the taste of real home cooking. The potatoes are soft and flaky and the onions thick and chunky. I like my onions sliced thickly to retain their bite and texture.

1   Peel the potatoes and chop them evenly as you would for roast potatoes. Soak in water for 5–6 minutes to remove any excess starch, then drain.

2   Cut the onion into 6 wedge-shaped pieces, then chop the beef into bite-size pieces.

3   Heat the oil in a large saucepan. Stir-fry the potatoes, add the onions and beef and cook for a few minutes.

4   Add the dashi stock, soy sauce, sugar, mirin and sake to the saucepan and simmer. Skim the surface and then place a drop lid on top. Simmer until the potatoes are cooked.

5   Taste before serving. If you want a richer flavor, add some soy sauce and extra sugar. Serve in bowls.

SERVES 4

1²/₃ cups potatoes
1 large onion
¹/₂ lb. finely sliced beef
1 tablespoon sunflower or vegetable oil
2 cups dashi stock or light fish stock
¹/₃ cup soy sauce
3 tablespoons superfine sugar
2 tablespoons mirin
1 tablespoon sake

Harumi's Hint

A drop lid is traditionally a wooden lid that is placed on top of cooking food in the saucepan. It enables the ingredients to cook evenly in stock or broth. These days I use drop lids made from a circle of foil or wax paper. Cut the lid slightly smaller then the pan that you are using so it fits inside and make a small hole in the center to allow steam to escape (see page 16).

Beef and Potato Croquettes

Croquettes are really popular in Japan. They are made with all sorts of different fillings and served up as part of lunch or dinner or even in bento (lunch boxes). From childhood, I have always particularly enjoyed beef and potato croquettes. I love the contrast between their crispy outside and soft filling. I also like making them in different shapes, depending on my mood. Whichever shape you choose, they should be served up, as with tonkatsu, with finely shredded cabbage. The addition of basil or shiso leaves to the cabbage gives this classic recipe an unusual aromatic twist.

SERVES 4

1²/₃ lbs. potatoes
¹/₂ lb. onions
²/₃ lb. minced beef
salt and pepper
2³/₄ tablespoons butter
all-purpose flour, beaten egg and breadcrumbs,
    for dipping and coating
sunflower or vegetable oil—for deep-frying
basil—to taste
cabbage, shredded—to taste
tonkatsu sauce—to taste

Harumi's Hint

As this mixture is quite soft, be careful that the croquettes don't break up while cooking and turn them with care once they start to brown, ensuring an even color. The quantity of breadcrumbs needed depends on the size of croquettes, however as a rough rule of thumb, you need about ¹/₃ cup of breadcrumbs for this recipe.

1 Wash the potatoes in their skins. Cut in half and wrap in plastic wrap. Microwave on medium for about 9 minutes. If they are still hard, cook a little longer. Peel while hot and then mash until smooth.

2 Cut the onions into ¹/₃-inch square pieces. Lightly season the beef with salt and pepper. Heat the butter in a frying pan, add the beef and quickly fry. Add the onions and continue to fry until the onions are translucent.

3 Add the cooked beef mixture and its juices to the mashed potato. Season with salt and pepper and mix together well.

4 At this point you can, if you like, divide the mixture into 2 portions and use half for a croquette pie and the other half for individual

croquettes, or you can use it all to make the croquettes.

5 Take the mixture and shape into individual balls (see photo), dust with flour, dip in the beaten egg and then finally coat with the breadcrumbs.

6 Heat the oil to 340°F and deep-fry in batches until crispy.

7 Shred the basil leaves just before serving and mix with the finely shredded cabbage. Serve the croquettes next to the cabbage and basil mix. It is very popular to drizzle a little tonkatsu sauce over before eating.

Croquette Pie

This is great served with a fresh green salad for breakfast or as a weekend brunch.

1 To make the pastry case: Chill all the ingredients and the bowl in the fridge before starting. Once cool, take out of the fridge and add the flour and butter to the chilled bowl. Using a palette knife or spoon, cut up the butter in the flour and then rub the butter into the flour with your fingertips until it resembles breadcrumbs. This should be done as quickly as possible for a light and crumbly result. Add a little salt and then the beaten egg.

2 Shape the dough into a ball. Cover with plastic wrap and let it rest in the fridge.

3 Sprinkle flour onto a board, place the pastry onto it and roll it out to just slightly larger than your flan tin. Place the pastry in the tin and trim the edges. Allow it to rest in the fridge. Meanwhile, preheat the oven to 350–400°F.

4 Prick the pastry with a fork and cover the base with a circle of wax paper. Bake for 15 minutes. Remove the paper and continue cooking for an additional 8 minutes. Remove and leave the oven on.

5 To make the croquette pie: Warm the beef and potato croquette mixture in the microwave, if cold. Fill the hot pastry case with the mix, sprinkle with breadcrumbs and flecks of butter. Bake in the oven for 10 minutes until warmed through. Halfway through cooking, check and cover with foil if it is overcooking at the edges.

6 When cooked, take out of the oven and remove from the tin. Serve with a choice of ketchup, tonkatsu sauce, mayonnaise or mustard.

You will need an 8-inch diameter pie or flan tin. For the pastry case:

1¹/2 cups all-purpose flour

¹/3 cup unsalted butter, cut into ¹/3-inch cubes

¹/3 teaspoon salt

1 egg

a little flour for dusting

¹/2 amount of the beef and potato mixture from the croquette recipe

2 tablespoons breadcrumbs

1 tablespoon butter

ketchup, tonkatsu sauce, mayonnaise and mustard—to serve

Fish & Seafood

Sashimi

The major difference between Japan's two most famous dishes, sushi and sashimi, is that the fish in sashimi is always raw and is not placed on top of rice. Sashimi is probably the ultimate Japanese dish, completely reliant on the basic guidelines of freshness and variety.

In most capital cities in the world you will find Japanese specialty shops that sell fish of sashimi quality. I would strongly recommend that you buy your sashimi fish from them. However, if you cannot, then go to a fish market with an excellent reputation for freshness.

Any fish you buy should not smell fishy. The eyes should be bright, the gills clean and the flesh should not be at all sticky. There is a question about parasites in freshwater fish, so try to buy saltwater fish instead. If you have any doubts, please do not use it for sashimi.

Sashimi can be a work of art so present it on a plate to enhance its beauty. Ensure you have dishes for soy sauce and wasabi; the sashimi is then dipped into this mix. If you can find daikon (Japanese mooli) you can shred it for use under the cut sashimi (see opposite). It not only helps with the presentation but it is also a very tasty accompaniment, as are shiso leaves. Remember, the tougher the fish the more finely it should be sliced. You can serve sashimi as a starter or as a main course with white rice and a miso shiru.

Tuna Sashimi in a Miso Dressing

This is a variation on a theme. Sashimi can be served in so many simple ways, here with a tasty miso dressing. It is particularly good in spring and works well as a side dish. You can also add ikura (salmon roe) if you like, for a richer flavor.

SERVES 2–3

1/3 lb. sashimi-quality raw tuna—medium fat (chu toro)

1 1/2 cups wakegi (if available) or chives or spring onions

3 tablespoons red miso

1 1/2 tablespoons superfine sugar

1/2 tablespoon mirin

1 teaspoon rice vinegar

a little mustard—to taste

1 tablespoon freshly grated ginger—to serve

1 Cut the tuna into 3/4-inch-square cubes. In a small pan, lightly boil the wakegi and leave to cool, then cut into 1- to 1 1/2-inch pieces.

2 In a bowl, mix together the miso, sugar, mirin, rice vinegar and mustard, then gently fold in the tuna, making sure it's well coated with the dressing.

3 Arrange in a serving bowl and garnish with the grated ginger.

Ingredients Note

Sashimi-quality tuna comes in different grades of fattiness; the most highly sought-after cut being o-toro—the fattiest—followed by chu-toro—medium fat.

Wakegi is a type of spring onion that is often used in soups in Japanese cooking. When it is boiled it can become a little slimy, which we remove by running a knife down it.

Harumi's Tuna Tataki Salad

Tataki is one of the most popular ways of cooking meat or fish: quickly seared on high heat and served almost raw with a variety of condiments and dipping sauces. As you can see in the photo, this tataki salad offers a great variety of tastes and textures and is also beautiful to look at. Use your own creativity to create attractive-looking dishes.

SERVES 4

1/3 lb. sashimi-quality raw tuna (chu toro—medium fat)
salt
sunflower or vegetable oil

Suggested ingredients for serving:
finely sliced onion, julienned cucumber, carrot, daikon (mooli or Japanese white radish)—all in 1 1/4-inch lengths and soaked in ice-cold water before patting dry
shredded shiso leaves or a mix of fresh mint and basil, benitade, hojiso (see Ingredients Note)
ikura (salmon roe)
salt, pepper, olive oil, Parmesan cheese
sudachi or lemon/lime juice

Ingredients Note
Benitade is a plant with small purple leaves and a peppery flavor. The leaves are often mixed into soy sauce together with wasabi and used as a dip for sashimi.

Another common flavoring is hojiso, the stems of young budding shiso plants. The emerging buds are scraped off the stem and added to the dipping sauce. (See page 90, bottom right, for photos of these plants with sashimi.)

1 Season the tuna with salt. In a frying pan, heat a little oil on high heat. Add the tuna to the pan, quickly sear, then remove and set aside.

2 Arrange a selection of the suggested vegetables in small dishes. Slice the tuna and place on top of the vegetables. Dress with any of the suggested toppings and season with salt, pepper, cheese, olive oil and sudachi to taste.

Checked-Top Sushi

I created this recipe for the Japanese Girls' Day Festival, which is held on March 3. It is always fun to make a special meal for your children but this variation of sushi is also really popular with adults. It is a little time-consuming to prepare but the blend of flavors is fantastic and it always looks stunning.

SERVES 4

For the sushi rice:
2¼ cups uncooked Japanese rice
2½ cups water
½ cup sushi rice vinegar

For the beef mixture:
¼ lb. finely sliced beef
¼ cup carrots
4 dried shiitake mushrooms
1½ tablespoons soy sauce
1 tablespoon sake
1 tablespoon mirin
2 teaspoons superfine sugar

For the thin crepe:
2 eggs
1 teaspoon superfine sugar
½ teaspoon sake
light soy sauce
sunflower or vegetable oil

Toppings:
sashimi-quality raw fish (medium fatty tuna), white fish, squid and scallops
chopped mitsuba or coriander
wasabi and soy sauce—to taste

1 To make the sushi rice: Wash the rice and cook with an equal amount of water so the rice is a little harder than usual and therefore more suitable for making sushi rice.

2 To make the beef mixture: Cut the beef into 1-inch square pieces. Chop the carrots into thick 1-inch-long batons. Soak the dried shiitake mushrooms in warm water until soft, then lightly squeeze to remove any excess water. Reserve 2 tablespoons of the water. Discard the mushroom stalks and then finely slice.

3 In a small nonstick pan, quickly fry the beef then add the reserved water from the mushrooms, the soy sauce, sake, mirin and sugar. Bring to a boil, add the carrots and mushrooms and simmer until the liquid has evaporated.

4 To finish the sushi rice: Gently mix the hot cooked rice with the sushi vinegar, taking care not to break the rice grains as you mix them. While the rice is still hot, add the cooked beef mixture and carefully mix together.

5 To make the crepe: In a bowl, beat the eggs and mix with the sugar, sake and light soy sauce. Heat a little oil in a frying pan, removing any excess with a paper towel. Pour just enough egg mix to thinly coat the bottom of the pan to make a thin crepe. Cook until done but not crispy. Repeat as before until all mixture is used. Leave to cool and slice into thin strips.

6 With a sharp knife, score the squid in a lattice pattern. Chop the squid, tuna, white fish and scallops into bite-size pieces.

7 Shape the beef and sushi rice mixture into small box shapes each suitable for one person. Arrange the fish and strips of crepe on top and garnish with mitsuba leaves, soy sauce and wasabi.

Grilled Aromatic Mackerel

Mackerel is a wonderful fish full of flavor and goodness, and this recipe provides an easy and tasty way to cook it. Who could resist the glorious aromas and colors?

SERVES 4

2 tablespoons mirin
2 tablespoons superfine sugar
2 tablespoons soy sauce
1 tablespoon rice vinegar
1 tablespoon kochujan (see Ingredients Note)
1 tablespoon ginger, peeled and thinly sliced
1⅓ lbs. fresh mackerel fillets
3–4 cabbage leaves
½ cup butter
salt and pepper
chopped spring onions or chives——to serve

1 In a bowl, make a marinade by mixing together the mirin, sugar, soy sauce, rice vinegar, kochujan and ginger.

2 Cut each mackerel fillet into 3 pieces on the diagonal. Lightly season with salt and leave for 5 minutes, then pat dry. Place in the marinade and set aside for about 30 minutes. Preheat the oven to 450°F.

3 Line a baking tray with wax paper or foil and place the drained mackerel pieces skin side up. Place into the oven and bake for 15 minutes.

4 In the meantime, cut the cabbage into bite-size pieces. In a frying pan, melt the butter and quickly fry the cabbage. Season with salt and pepper.

5 Once cooked, remove the mackerel from the oven.

6 Place the cooked cabbage on a serving dish with the mackerel on top. Serve with plenty of chopped spring onions or chives sprinkled on top.

Ingredients Note

Kochujan is spicy Korean miso paste. You can substitute a mixture of red miso and chili paste. Add the chili paste gradually until it is to your own liking.

Prawns in Chili Sauce

Ebi Chili Sauce

Originally a Chinese dish, this has been well adapted to suit the taste of the Japanese and is now served up in almost every household in Japan. It is one of the recipes most requested by my readers. Use jumbo king prawns for the best results.

SERVES 4

12 fresh king prawns (around 1 oz. each)
a little salt, pepper, shokoshu (or dry sherry) and
    sesame oil—to marinate
2 tablespoons sunflower or vegetable oil
1 cup spring onions, roughly chopped
1 tablespoon finely chopped fresh ginger
1/2 tablespoon finely chopped fresh garlic
1/2–1 tablespoon chili paste or to-ban-jan—to taste
2 tablespoons potato starch or corn starch mixed
    with 2 tablespoons water
1 tablespoon sesame oil

For the sauce:

1 cup hot water
1 teaspoon granulated chicken stock powder
6 tablespoons ketchup
1 tablespoon shokoshu or dry sherry
2 teaspoons superfine sugar
salt
1 tablespoon rice vinegar

Menu Planning

This is lovely with Japanese rice, bok choy, pickles and a soup, such the Clear Soup with Pork and Spinach Wonton Dumplings (see page 28).

1   First remove the head, shell and tail of the prawns, then devein by bending each prawn and, using a toothpick, carefully pulling out the dark vein. Marinate in a mixture of salt, pepper, shokoshu and sesame oil.

2   To make the sauce: In a bowl mix together the hot water, chicken stock powder, ketchup, shokoshu, sugar, salt and rice vinegar.

3   In a wok, heat the oil, add the chopped spring onions, ginger and garlic and quickly fry. When the aroma is released, add the chili paste.

4   Now add the prawns and fry quickly. Add the sauce and bring to a boil. Then add the potato starch to thicken. Finally add the sesame oil, which will enhance the aroma, and serve immediately.

Japanese-Style Squid Salad

We eat a lot of squid in Japan. In fact, I think we probably eat more squid than any other seafood. The ginger and soy sauce in this dressing give this simple salad a real Japanese flavor.

SERVES 4
1¹/₂ lbs. fresh squid
salt and pepper
2 tablespoons olive oil
2¹/₂ teaspoons crushed garlic (1 clove)
mixed salad leaves—to taste
chili powder or shichimi togarashi—to taste

For the dressing:
3 tablespoons soy sauce
1 tablespoon freshly grated ginger
superfine sugar—to taste

1   To prepare the squid: Remove the guts and legs from the body and rinse. Discard the tips of the legs and chop the remaining leg pieces into bite-size chunks. Cut the body into ¹/₂-inch-thick rings. Season with salt and pepper.

2   Heat the olive oil in a frying pan and fry the garlic. Once you can smell its aroma, add the squid and cook until done. Turn off the heat and immediately remove the squid and set aside.

3   To make the dressing: In the same frying pan, add the soy sauce, ginger and sugar and mix well with any remaining cooking juices, making sure that the sugar dissolves.

4   Tear the salad leaves into bite-size pieces. Soak in water with ice cubes to crisp up. Drain, pat dry and put in a serving dish. Place the squid on top, pour over the dressing and sprinkle some chili powder or shichimi togarashi, to taste, on top.

Harumi's Hint
To ensure that the squid remains tender, remove from the frying pan as soon as it is cooked. Do not leave it in the pan or it will continue cooking and become tough.

Lightly Pickled Mackerel, Japanese Style

Shime Saba

This is a much simpler and easier dish than you might imagine. Although it's a traditional New Year dish I make it all year round, as it is one of my husband's favorites. You must ensure that the mackerel is absolutely fresh for this recipe but you can grill any leftovers the following day.

SERVES 4

1¹/₃ lbs. mackerel fillets
4–6 tablespoons salt
3/4 cup rice vinegar
2 tablespoons superfine sugar
light soy sauce
1 cup spring onions
10 shiso leaves or a mix of fresh mint and basil
soy sauce, mustard or wasabi—to taste

1 Using fish tweezers, remove any bones from the mackerel, taking care not to break up the flesh. Sprinkle 1–1¹/₂ tablespoons of salt on each side of the fish and leave for about 2 hours. Then carefully wash off the salt under running water and pat dry.

2 In a non-aluminum container, combine the rice vinegar, sugar and light soy sauce. Place the mackerel fillets in this marinade and leave for about 30 minutes, turning occasionally.

3 Finely slice the spring onions, soak in water to remove any sharpness and then pat dry. Shred the shiso leaves.

4 Carefully remove the transparent membrane from the fish skin and discard. Slice the fish thickly. Arrange on a serving dish with the spring onions and shredded shiso leaves and serve with small dishes of dipping sauce. Soy sauce with mustard or wasabi is a tasty accompaniment.

Flaked Mackerel with Vegetables

Saba Soboro

I have been eating my mother's Flaked Mackerel with Vegetables since I was a little girl. She usually uses horse mackerel, which has a slightly different flavor, but for my version I use regular mackerel. It's a great recipe, as you can cook the fish together with the vegetables using just one pan. It is also very versatile and you can use the flakes on hot rice or cold in a bento (lunch box).

SERVES 2–4
1/2 lb. fresh mackerel fillets
3/4 cup onions
1/4 cup carrots
1/4 cup (3–4) dried shiitake mushrooms
1 tablespoon fresh ginger, peeled
1–2 tablespoons sunflower or vegetable oil
1 tablespoon sake
1 tablespoon superfine sugar
2 tablespoons mirin
4 tablespoons soy sauce

1 Using a spoon and starting at the head, scrape the mackerel flesh from its skin. Roughly chop up the flesh and put aside.
2 Finely dice the onions and carrots. Soak the dried shiitake mushrooms in water until soft, lightly squeeze dry, then remove the stems and roughly chop the flesh. Finely chop the ginger.
3 Heat the oil in a frying pan and fry the mackerel and ginger. Once the mackerel turns opaque, flake the flesh and add the chopped onions, carrots and shiitake mushrooms, mixing well.
4 Add the sake, sugar, mirin and soy sauce and simmer, stirring from time to time until all the liquid has evaporated. If you want a richer dish, reduce the amount of soy sauce and add instead 1/2 tablespoon of miso and 1 tablespoon of sake.

SERVES 2

2 eggs, beaten

2 teaspoons superfine sugar

1 teaspoon sake

salt

sunflower or vegetable oil

7–8 snow peas

1 3/4 cups cooked rice

1 cup cooked mackerel mix (see opposite)

Japanese pickles (see page 126)—to serve

Flaked Mackerel with Vegetables on Rice Saba Soboro Gohan

This dish is very popular with children (and men, too!). Serve with a selection of Japanese pickles and a topping such as crumbled nori seaweed (ao nori).

1 Mix the eggs with the sugar, sake and salt. Heat a little oil in a frying pan and cook as you would scrambled eggs.

2 Lightly cook the snow peas, drain and cut diagonally into small pieces.

3 Divide the cooked rice between 2 plates or bowls and then spoon the mackerel mix and some scrambled eggs on top. Garnish with the snow peas. Serve with your favorite Japanese pickles.

Appetizer of Squid, Japanese Style

In this lovely recipe tender pieces of squid are mixed with a tasty, sweet dressing. It makes an unusual appetizer for a special meal or can be served as a side dish.

SERVES 4
¼ lb. sashimi-quality raw squid
10 shiso leaves or a mix of fresh mint and basil
4 kabosu or limes—hollowed-out to use as
    serving dishes

For the pickled plum dressing:
1 tablespoon plum paste (bainiku) (see Ingredients
    Note)
½ tablespoon mirin
½ teaspoon soy sauce
freshly grated daikon (mooli or Japanese white
    radish)—to taste

Ingredients Note
It is becoming much easier to find plum paste
(bainiku) but you can always make your own plum
paste by mashing up the flesh of large soft
umeboshi plums (remove the pits first).

1   Make sure that you buy squid that is suitable for sashimi, i.e., extremely fresh and well cleaned with no guts. Slice the body of the squid lengthways to make fine, thin ribbons.
2   Finely chop the shiso leaves.
3   To make the dressing: In a bowl, mix the plum paste with the mirin and soy sauce. Adjust the amounts to taste according to the saltiness of the plum paste.
4   Combine the squid with the dressing and then lightly mix in the chopped shiso leaves.
5   Serve in the hollowed-out lime halves, garnished with grated daikon.

How to make citrus fruit dishes for the table:
I like using scooped-out citrus fruits to serve food like this. You can use these citrus cups for serving a variety of delicacies, both savory and sweet, or even as a sake cup.

1   Cut the fruit in half or to the required size. Take a little off the bottom, making sure not to make a hole, to help the cup stand.
2   Run a knife around the inside edge, between the skin and the pulp, then remove the pulp using a spoon. (You can keep the pulp and use it later for another recipe.)
3   You can prepare these cups a day in advance. If you do so, keep the scooped-out cups wrapped in damp paper towels and plastic wrap in the fridge.

Japanese-Style Sardines with Pickled Plums

Fresh sardines not only look lovely but are also really delicious. In this recipe I prepare them with two very Japanese flavors, ginger and umeboshi (pickled plums). It is a wonderful combination of tastes and aromas.

1 Ask your fishmonger to clean the sardines and remove the heads. At home wash them well and cut each one in half across the fish, not lengthways.

2 Peel and chop the ginger into julienne.

3 In a large frying pan or sauté pan, mix the soy sauce, sake, mirin and sugar and bring to a boil. Place the sardines in the pan side by side with the umeboshi on top. Sprinkle over the ginger.

4 Make a drop lid using foil or wax paper and place it in the pan, on top of the sardines. Simmer until cooked, occasionally basting the fish with the juices.

5 Serve immediately in small bowls with the chopped kinome sprinkled on top.

SERVES 4

8 fresh large sardines (each fish weighing about 1/3 lb.)
1 tablespoon fresh ginger
1/2 cup soy sauce
1/3 cup sake
1/3 cup mirin
3 tablespoons superfine sugar
3 umeboshi (see Ingredients Note)
chopped kinome or spring onion—to taste

Ingredients Note
Umeboshi, often referred to as pickled plums, are actually apricots. There are two types—small and hard, large and soft—and it's these large ones that you need for this recipe. It's difficult to achieve the correct result without umeboshi, so do try to get ahold of them.

Poached Red Sea Bream

When I am in Japan I make this recipe with a fish called kinmedai, which is closely associated with the town of Shimoda, where I grew up. However, it might be hard to find outside Japan so here I have substituted red sea bream, which has a similar flavor. The tasty sauce was created by my mother. My contribution was to cut the fish into chunks and serve it with seaweed and burdock.

SERVES 4
1 lb. red sea bream fillets
$\frac{1}{4}$ cup sake
$\frac{1}{4}$ cup mirin
$\frac{1}{4}$ cup soy sauce
$\frac{1}{4}$ cup water
3 tablespoons superfine sugar
1 tablespoon fresh ginger, sliced
8-inch piece dried wakame seaweed
cooked burdock (see below)

For the cooked burdock:

SERVES 4
2 cups burdock
1 tablespoon sunflower or vegetable oil
2 tablespoons soy sauce
2 tablespoons mirin
1 tablespoon sake
2 teaspoons superfine sugar

1 Cut each fish fillet into 3–4 pieces.
2 In a large shallow pan, mix together the sake, mirin, soy sauce, water and sugar and bring it to a boil. Add the fish pieces into the broth, taking care to arrange them so they sit side by side. Sprinkle the sliced ginger over the fish.
3 Bring back to a boil, cover with a drop lid made from foil or wax paper and simmer for 5–6 minutes. When the liquid has reduced to just less than half, turn off the heat and leave for a short while for the fish to absorb some of the remaining liquid.
4 Soak the wakame seaweed in water until soft. Drain and squeeze it to remove any excess water and then roughly chop.
5 Remove the fish and ginger from the pan and place on a serving dish alongside the seaweed and burdock. Pour over any remaining sauce from the pan.

Cooked Burdock

1 Peel the burdock and cut into 2- to 2½-inch length julienne. Soak in water for 5–10 minutes. Drain and pat dry.
2 Heat the oil in a frying pan. Add the burdock and quickly stir-fry. Add the soy sauce, mirin, sake and sugar and mix together, cooking until the liquid has evaporated. Remove from heat.

Grilled Salmon "Yuan" Style

Sake no Yuan Yaki

This marinade is similar to teriyaki but the yuzu adds a distinctive flavor. You can use it for most types of fish. The grilled fish can be eaten either hot or cold and is a common addition to bento (lunch boxes).

SERVES 4

¹/₄ cup sake
¹/₄ cup mirin
¹/₂ cup soy sauce
half a yuzu or lemon, sliced
4 x ¹/₄-lb. salmon fillets, each cut into
  3 pieces, bones removed
sudachi or lemon/lime—to taste

Ingredient Notes

Japanese cuisine makes great use of the various citrus fruits available. Yuzu is a yellow citrus with a very delicate aroma. Its zest is used to flavor many popular dishes such as yudofu. Sudachi is similar to yuzu but smaller and sharper. They are sometimes available outside of Japan but if you can't find them, substitute a lemon or lime.

1 In a large dish mix the sake, mirin, soy sauce and yuzu, and marinate the salmon for at least 3–4 hours.

2 Remove the salmon from the marinade. Place under a hot grill until just cooked. Serve with wedges of sudachi.

Cod Roe with Noodles

Tarako or salted cod roe is quite salty and has a strong flavor. You can serve this dish either hot or cold—it is sometimes used in bento (lunch boxes). It's also a perfect opportunity to try out your cooking chopsticks technique!

SERVES 4

7 oz. shirataki noodles or thin vermicelli-style noodles

2 tablespoons salted cod roe (tarako)

1¼ cups mitsuba or coriander stems

2 teaspoons mirin

1 tablespoon light soy sauce

light soy sauce—to taste

1 Wash the shirataki noodles, boil for 5–6 minutes, then drain well and cut into easy-to-eat lengths.

2 Remove the membrane from around the cod roe and scrape out the required amount of roe using a spoon.

3 Remove the leaves from the mitsuba and cut the stems into 1½-inch pieces. (You can save the leaves to use in another recipe.) Parboil the stems, then chill in cold water. Drain and squeeze to remove excess water.

4 Pat dry the shirataki noodles, put in a wok or a frying pan and heat without adding any oil. Add the mirin and soy sauce and cook for a couple of minutes, then turn off the heat and immediately add the cod roe. Stir using cooking chopsticks and leave to cool slightly.

5 Lightly mix in the mitsuba stems, season with light soy sauce and serve.

Harumi's Hint

You can substitute the shirataki noodles with either thin vermicelli-style noodles or with Japanese dried harusame noodles.

Ingredients Note

Light soy sauce is saltier than dark soy sauce. Japanese soy sauce is also slightly different in flavor from other Asian soy sauces. Where possible, use Japanese soy sauce for these recipes.

Vegetables

Two Types of Mini Tempura

Mini Kakiage

Tempura is a style of deep-frying in a light batter. You can make tempura with many kinds of ingredients. If you are looking for an interesting way to serve vegetables, tempura is perfect. Here are two different forms of tempura that you can serve as side dishes, or as an addition to another dish such as the Soba Chirashi (see page 56).

SERVES 2

For the shrimp and spring onion tempura:

4 oz. fresh-shelled shrimp

1 cup spring onions

1/4 cup + 1 extra tablespoon tempura flour
(see Ingredients Note)

3 tablespoons ice water

sunflower or vegetable oil—for deep-frying

For the carrot and burdock tempura:

1/4 cup carrots

1/4 cup burdock

1/4 cup + 1 extra tablespoon tempura flour
(see Ingredients Note)

3 tablespoons cold water

sunflower or vegetable oil—for deep-frying

Ingredients Note

Tempura flour or tempura ko is a ready-made mix containing dried egg, and is a quick and foolproof way of making tempura batter. Just by adding water you are guaranteed delicious, crispy results every time. Or you can make your own batter mix. You may have to experiment a little, depending on the flour available in your country.

Basic Tempura Batter: 2 1/4 cups self-rising flour (or a mix of all-purpose flour and corn starch), 1 egg yolk and 1/2 cup ice water. When you are ready to start cooking, lightly mix the egg yolk into the ice water and then add that to the flour and mix lightly. Do not over mix—it should be lumpy. Use immediately.

Shrimp and Spring Onion Tempura:

1 Wash the shrimp and devein if necessary. Cut the spring onions into 1- to 1 1/2-inch pieces.

2 Put the shrimp and spring onions in a bowl, add the 1/4 cup of tempura flour and the cold water, and mix lightly. Add the remaining tablespoon of tempura flour and lightly combine once more.

3 In a wok or a saucepan, heat the oil to 340°F. Divide the mix into 4 batches. Deep-fry 2 batches of tempura at a time and serve hot.

Carrot and Burdock Tempura:

1 Peel and slice the carrots and burdock diagonally and then cut into fine strips of equal sizes. Soak the burdock in water for 2–3 minutes, drain and pat dry.

2 Place the carrots and burdock in a bowl with 1/4 cup of the tempura flour and the water and lightly mix. Then add the remaining tablespoon of flour and lightly combine once more.

3 In a wok or a saucepan heat the oil to 340°F. Divide the mix into 4 batches. Cook 2 batches at a time and serve hot.

Daikon and Carrots with a Korean-Style Dressing

Daikon to Ninjin no Namuru

This is a simple but tasty side salad. If you have never tried daikon before, now is the time to do so! It is a well-loved, well-used vegetable in Japanese cuisine. You can serve it grated, on top or on the side of grilled or deep-fried foods, cooked in stews or just julienned raw, as in this salad.

SERVES 4

2¹/₃ cups daikon (mooli or Japanese white radish)
¹/₂ cup carrots
¹/₂ teaspoon salt
3 tablespoons finely chopped spring onions
1 tablespoon finely chopped garlic
1¹/₃ tablespoons granulated chicken stock powder
2 tablespoons rice vinegar
2 teaspoons superfine sugar
salt
2 tablespoons sesame oil
coarsely ground toasted white sesame seeds

1 Peel the daikon and carrots and cut into 2¹/₂-inch-length julienne.
2 Toss the daikon and carrots in the salt and leave until slightly softened. Squeeze to remove any excess water.
3 In a bowl, combine the daikon and carrot with the finely chopped spring onions and garlic. Add the following ingredients in order, combining well before adding the next: chicken stock powder, rice vinegar, sugar, salt and sesame oil. Toss with plenty of sesame seeds, arrange in a dish and serve immediately.

Sautéed Bean Sprouts with Bok Choy

This is so simple and combines two of my favorite vegetables: bok choy and bean sprouts. Again, I strongly recommend that you do trim the tops and bottoms of the bean sprouts—they really do taste better! You can serve this dish with almost any of the recipes in this book, for lunch or dinner.

SERVES 4–6
1/2 cup bok choy
4 cups bean sprouts
2 tablespoons sunflower or vegetable oil
2 cloves garlic, finely sliced
1 teaspoon granulated chicken stock powder
soy sauce
1 tablespoon sesame oil

1 Chop the bok choy into 3–4 pieces. Separate the leaves from the stems and cut the stems into 2–3 pieces lengthways. Trim the bean sprouts.
2 Heat the oil in a frying pan and fry the garlic. As soon as the aroma is released, add the bok choy stems, quickly fry and then add the bean sprouts. Continue cooking for a minute or so and then sprinkle on the chicken stock powder.
3 Finally add the bok choy leaves and stir-fry briefly. Season with soy sauce and sesame oil.

Harumi's Hint
It is important to stir-fry the vegetables quickly over a high heat and not leave them for too long, as they will lose their natural juiciness and become soggy.

Eggplant and Harusame Noodle Salad

In this salad, steamed eggplant and harusame noodles are combined in a spicy dressing. This eggplant dish makes a delicious accompaniment to both meat and fish. Although it contains harusame noodles, you may still need to serve it with some rice.

SERVES 4

3/4 lb. eggplant
1/2 cup dried harusame noodles or vermicelli rice
   noodles (see Glossary)
coriander leaves—to taste

For the dressing:

1/2 teaspoon granulated chicken stock powder
   dissolved in 3 tablespoons hot water
2 1/2 tablespoons soy sauce
1 tablespoon superfine sugar
1 tablespoon sesame oil
1 teaspoon rice vinegar
2 teaspoons finely chopped ginger
1 red chili, sliced

Harumi's Hint

Soaking the eggplant in water removes any bitterness and stops the flesh from discoloring. Steaming the eggplant before cooking gives a smooth and juicy texture.

1 Remove the stem of the eggplant and peel. Cut in half horizontally and chop in quarters lengthways. If the eggplant is very large, chop further into smaller pieces. Soak in cold water for 5–6 minutes (see Harumi's Hint).

2 Cook the noodles according to the package instructions, taking care not to overcook. Cool in cold water, drain and roughly chop.

3 Place the eggplant in a steamer and cook for about 5 minutes until soft. Remove from the steamer and leave to cool.

4 To make the dressing: Add the soy sauce, sugar, sesame oil, rice vinegar, ginger and chili to the dissolved chicken stock and combine.

5 When the eggplant is cool enough to handle, cut each piece into 4 equal lengths. Lightly squeeze to remove excess liquid and place on a serving dish. Arrange the harusame noodles on top and pour the dressing over the noodles. Garnish with the coriander leaves.

Mixed Salad with Sesame Dressing

You can use this lovely creamy sesame dressing with most salads or with crudités. Once made, it will keep in the fridge for 2–3 days.

SERVES 4
a good selection of mixed salad leaves

For the sesame dressing:
2 tablespoons sesame paste (if available) or
    unsalted smooth peanut butter
2 tablespoons ground toasted white sesame seeds
2 tablespoons dashi stock
1 tablespoon rice vinegar
1 tablespoon soy sauce
1 tablespoon superfine sugar
salt and chili powder or shichimi togarashi—to taste

1 Tear the salad leaves into bite-size pieces and soak in water with ice cubes to crisp up. Drain and pat dry.
2 Combine all the ingredients for the dressing, mixing well.
3 Place the salad leaves in a suitable bowl and either serve the dressing separately or dress just before eating.

Potato Salad, Japanese Style

You can find potato salad everywhere in Japan, not only at home but also in bento (lunch boxes) or even as a filling for sandwiches! If I am only making a small amount I use the microwave to cook the potatoes and carrots, but if I am making a lot I use a steamer. I think you get the best results by cooking the potatoes and carrots in their skins, unpeeled. This makes the vegetables taste fresh and gives them a good texture.

SERVES 4
1¹/₂ lbs. large potatoes
¹/₂ lb. large carrots
1 teaspoon granulated chicken stock powder
²/₃ cup cucumber
¹/₂ teaspoon salt
¹/₃ cup onion
1 cup mayonnaise
salt and coarsely ground pepper

Harumi's Hint
You can make this salad look even more interesting by serving it in individual portions, as in these photos. Slices of hard-boiled eggs not only look attractive but they also complement the potato salad.

1 Wash the potatoes and carrots but do not peel.
2 Place in a hot steamer and cook for about 25 minutes over medium heat, taking care to top up the water from time to time as needed. Prick the vegetables with a toothpick or skewer to see if cooked and remove when done.
3 Peel the potatoes and carrots while hot, and then transfer the potatoes to a bowl and roughly break up. Mix in the chicken stock powder and leave to cool. Chop the carrots in half lengthways and slice into ¹/₅-inch-thick semicircular pieces. You can make quarter-button shapes by chopping the halved carrot again lengthways before slicing.
4 Cut the cucumber in half lengthways and, using a spoon, remove the seeds. Cut each half again lengthways and then slice into ¹/₅-inch-thick pieces. In a separate bowl, sprinkle salt over the cucumber and leave for about 2–3 minutes to soften, then squeeze to remove excess liquid. Cut the onion in half, slice and soak in water to remove any bitterness, then drain and pat dry.
5 When the potato is cool, add the carrots, cucumber and onions and lightly mix. Stir in the mayonnaise, salt and pepper, and serve.

Warm Cabbage Salad

For this recipe, try to find cabbage that has been grown in spring. Spring cabbage is much more tender than the cabbage you find the rest of the year and it makes this recipe very special. The addition of dried fish flakes is very Japanese—we love these flakes and use them in many recipes.

SERVES 4

¹/₂ lb. new spring cabbage
1 tablespoon soy sauce
¹/₂ tablespoon mirin
a little squeezed sudachi or lemon/lime
dried fish flakes (katsuo bushi)—to taste

1 Cut the cabbage into bite-size pieces, parboil and drain. You want to make sure the cabbage is not too soft but neither should it be too raw. Soak in cold water for a couple of minutes, drain and squeeze to remove any excess water.

2 In a bowl, mix the soy sauce, mirin and squeezed sudachi. Squeeze the cabbage again and mix with the dressing.

3 Serve either in individual dishes or on one serving dish and garnish with dried fish flakes.

Apple and Radish Dressed with Miso Mayonnaise

In this recipe I have revised a classic Waldorf Salad to suit the Japanese palate. The dressing can be used for other salads but is best with crunchy, slightly sharp-tasting ingredients.

SERVES 4

For the miso mayonnaise dressing:
2 teaspoons saikyo miso (see Ingredients Note)
1/2 cup mayonnaise
1 tablespoon rice vinegar

2 1/2 tablespoons shelled walnuts
3/4 cup red apple
salt
2 1/2 cups radish

Ingredients Note
Saikyo miso is another regional speciality miso, this time from Kyoto. It's much sweeter and lighter than other miso. If you cannot obtain it, use 2 teaspoons of white miso mixed with a little superfine sugar instead.

1 In a bowl, combine the miso, mayonnaise and rice vinegar. Cook the walnuts uncovered in a microwave on very low heat for 1 1/2 minutes. Leave to cool and roughly chop.

2 Wash the apple complete with skin. Cut into 4 wedges, removing the core, then slice each wedge into 1/10-inch-thick pieces. Add a little salt to a bowl of water and soak the apple in the mixture to keep it from discoloring. Slice the radishes into 1/10-inch-thick round pieces.

3 Just before serving, drain the apple and pat dry. Then dress the apple and radish with the miso mayonnaise sauce. Arrange in a serving bowl and sprinkle the walnut pieces on top.

Eggplant "Dengaku" Style

This delicious, sweet miso mixture is very versatile and can be spread on many different foods before grilling, "Dengaku" style. To eat, use a small spoon.

SERVES 2

For the dengaku miso:

6 tablespoons hatcho miso (see Ingredients Note)
4 tablespoons sugar
4 tablespoons mirin
2 tablespoons sake

1 large eggplant (about 3 cups)
3 tablespoons sunflower or vegetable oil
toasted sesame seeds

1 To make the dengaku miso: In a small pan, combine the miso, sugar, mirin and sake. Place on medium heat and stir to combine. Once the mixture thickens, turn off the heat.

2 Cut the eggplant in half lengthways, and then run a knife around the inside of the eggplant, loosening the skin from the flesh. Score the flat surface with a lattice pattern.

3 Heat the oil in a frying pan and add the eggplant, flesh side down, and brown. Then turn over, loosely cover with foil and continue cooking until almost cooked.

4 Spread 2 tablespoons of the dengaku miso on each half of the eggplant. Cook under a preheated grill for about 5 minutes and sprinkle with toasted sesame seeds.

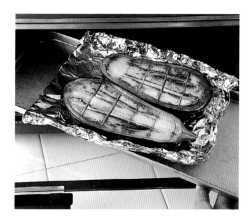

Ingredients Note

In Japan, you can find a great variety of miso, which differs from region to region. Hacho miso is a unique miso from Aichi Prefecture and is darker than regular misos. If you cannot find it, substitute red miso paste.

Japanese Pickles

Tsukemono

Pickles are served at almost every meal in Japan. You can buy many types of pickles from the supermarket but I like to make my own and keep a good stock available for meals with family and friends. They are surprisingly easy to make. In this recipe the vegetables are very lightly preserved.

SERVES 4

$^1/_2$ cup cucumber
$^2/_3$ cup carrots
4–5 cabbage leaves
1 tablespoon fresh ginger
1 teaspoon salt
$^1/_2$ tablespoon superfine sugar
1 tablespoon rice vinegar
dried fish flakes (katsuo bushi)
soy sauce or some ponzu soy sauce—to taste

1 Cut the cucumber in half lengthways and scoop out the seeds with a small spoon. Then cut it in half again lengthways and slice thinly. Peel the carrot and cut in half, then cut these halves into $1^1/_2$-inch-long pieces. Then take each $1^1/_2$-inch piece and finely slice, making thin rectangular shapes. Chop the cabbage into bite-size pieces. Peel the ginger and cut into strips.
2 In a container, mix the cucumber, carrots and cabbage leaves and sprinkle with the salt, sugar and rice vinegar. Put a plate on top and weight it down with something heavy like a paperweight or large food can. Leave for at least 10 hours or overnight.
3 Before serving, squeeze out any excess liquid by hand. Place in a small serving dish and sprinkle the dried fish flakes and ginger on top. Drizzle some soy sauce or ponzu soy sauce over top to taste.

Harumi's Hint

I use all sorts of vegetables like Chinese cabbage, mizuna, celery, radish or daikon for this recipe. I sometimes add chopped red chili, ginger, shiso leaves or even Western-style herbs. Be creative and make your own version!

Desserts & Drinks

White Chocolate Cake

This is an unusual cake as the white chocolate is not in the icing but in the cake itself, finely grated. This gives the cake a lovely texture and taste. I like to serve it for special occasions using different types of fruit on top.

SERVES 6
Use a 8 x 8 x 2 inch square baking pan or 7-inch diameter round pan

¼ cup good-quality white chocolate—leave in the fridge until ready to use

1 cup all-purpose flour

3 eggs

¼ cup granulated sugar

For the decoration:

¾ cup heavy or whipping cream

2 tablespoons granulated sugar

blueberries, mint leaves and powdered sugar, to decorate

Harumi's Hint

If you bake this cake in a round tin, you might want to cut the cake in half and fill with some of the cream mixture before spreading the remaining cream on top to decorate. You could also use a different fruit on each section to make it extra special.

1   Preheat the oven to 350°F. Line the pan with wax paper. Take the chocolate from the fridge and finely grate it using a cheese grater.

2   Sift the flour into a bowl and lightly mix in the grated chocolate.

3   In a separate bowl, beat the eggs then add the granulated sugar. Whisk until it stands in peaks. Stir in half the flour and chocolate mixture.

4   Then add the remaining flour to the bowl and lightly mix some more.

5   Transfer the mixture to the cake pan, tapping the pan on the work surface a few times to remove any air. Bake in the oven for about 20 minutes until lightly browned.

6   Remove from the oven and pan, place on a rack and leave to cool. While the cake is still slightly warm, wrap in plastic wrap and leave to cool completely (this keeps it from drying out).

7   To decorate: In a bowl, mix the cream and sugar then whisk until soft peaks are formed—do not overwhisk. Spread the cream mixture on top of the cake, decorate with blueberries and mint leaves, and sift powdered sugar over the top.

Harumi's Baked Cheesecake

Obviously, cheesecake is not a traditional Japanese dessert. However, it is now extremely popular in Japan and my readers love this particular recipe. It's very easy to make. I use graham crackers for the base and mix all the other ingredients in just one bowl. It's foolproof. When you take the cake out of the oven it is very light and soft like a soufflé, but once it has cooled down it becomes creamy and smooth. If you then refrigerate it, it becomes thick and rich. It is almost like having three different cakes.

SERVES 6

Use a 7-inch spring-form pan

1 cup graham cracker crumbs

3 tablespoons unsalted butter

1 cup cream cheese

1/2 cup granulated sugar

2 eggs

1 cup heavy cream

3 tablespoons sifted all-purpose flour

1 tablespoon lemon juice

1 Make sure the butter and cream cheese are at room temperature. Line the cake pan with wax paper.

2 Put the graham crackers in a plastic bag and roughly crush with a rolling pin.

3 Soften the butter and mix with the graham cracker crumbs.

4 Pour the graham cracker mix into the bottom of the pan and press down lightly to make the base. Preheat the oven to 340°F.

5 In a bowl, beat the cream cheese with an electric mixer until soft, then add the rest of the ingredients, in order, mixing each one thoroughly first before adding the next.

6 Continue until the mixture thickens, then pour into the cake pan, on top of the graham cracker base. Bake in the oven for 45–50 minutes. Remove and leave to cool.

7 Once it has cooled, remove from the pan, discard the lining paper and leave on a rack to cool completely.

Rice Dumplings with Mango Sauce

Mango Sauce no Shiratama

The flavors in this recipe are rooted in the various cuisines of Asia. We love the combination of dumplings, sweet beans and fruit. If you have never tried this before I strongly recommend it, especially after a spicy meal.

SERVES 4

For the rice dumplings:

1/3 cup shiratama ko (see Ingredients Note)
1/2 tablespoon superfine sugar
1/3 cup water
sweetened adzuki beans—to taste

For the mango sauce:

1 ripe mango (1 1/4 cups)
3–4 tablespoons superfine sugar
1 cup soy milk
1/2 cup coconut milk

1   To make the rice dumplings: In a bowl mix the shiratama ko and sugar using your hands. Add the water, bit by bit, and knead until the dough feels smooth and elastic. Form into small balls.

2   In a large pan, bring plenty of water to a boil, then add the rice balls and cook in small batches. When the balls rise to the surface, remove and soak in cold water. Transfer to a colander to drain well.

3   To make the mango sauce: Peel the mango, slice the flesh and mash roughly with a mortar and pestle. Add the sugar, soy milk and coconut milk and mix well.

4   Pour the mango sauce into a serving bowl and add the dumplings. Spoon the sweetened adzuki beans on top and serve. Delicious!

Ingredients Note

Shiratama ko is a Japanese type of glutinous rice flour. Regular rice flour does not produce a satisfactory result.

You can find ready-prepared adzuki beans at Japanese or Asian supermarkets but you can also easily prepare them yourself. Soak the adzuki beans overnight and then cook until soft. Add sugar to taste, stirring over low heat until the sugar has melted.

Baked Papaya with Coconut Milk

This is such a delicious and easy dessert. The color of the cooked papaya and the creamy sauce are delightful, as are the sweet flavors of the fruit, coconut and cream. A marriage of tastes made in heaven!

SERVES 4
1 whole fresh papaya (about 1½ lbs.)
½ cup coconut milk
¼ cup heavy cream
4 tablespoons condensed milk

1   Put the papaya on the work surface, keeping it stable—if you need to, cut off a little of the skin to help make it level. Cut a thick slice or wedge from the upper side of the fruit and keep to use as a lid later. Scoop out the seeds from the remaining section.

2   In a bowl, mix together the coconut milk, heavy cream and condensed milk. Pour into the hollowed-out papaya, taking care not to overfill.

3   Put the papaya lid back on and wrap in heat-resistant plastic wrap. Microwave on medium for about 5–6 minutes until the sauce is very hot. Remove carefully from the microwave.

4   Immediately take off the plastic wrap, carefully spoon out the papaya flesh and hot sauce into small bowls and serve.

Green Tea Ice Cream

Macha Ice

When I visit Japanese restaurants abroad, I often find this dish on the dessert menu. There has been a huge growth in interest in green tea outside of Japan and I find it makes a great gift for my friends overseas. The green color of this homemade ice cream is beautiful and the aroma heavenly.

SERVES 4

2 tablespoons green tea powder (macha)

²/₃ cup granulated sugar

3 egg yolks

3/4 cup milk

3/4 cup heavy cream

1 In a small bowl, mix the green tea powder with 2 tablespoons granulated sugar.

2 In a separate bowl, mix together the egg yolks and remaining sugar.

3 Pour the milk into a small pan and gently heat taking care not to let it boil (ideally the temperature of the milk should be 176°F). Remove from the heat and mix a few spoonfuls of the warm milk with the green tea powder and sugar in a small bowl. When you have a smooth paste, add it to the remaining milk in the pan, then gradually combine with the egg yolks mixture. Leave to cool.

4 Lightly whip the cream and then add to the cold green tea–milk mixture.

5 Transfer the mixture to a large container and put in the freezer. As ice crystals start to form, remove, mix well with a spoon to break them up and return to the freezer. Repeat this a few times as it freezes to ensure that the ice cream is really smooth.

Drinks

I think the popular image of the Japanese is that we are rather serious all the time. I would like to dispel this illusion—we enjoy letting our hair down and having fun! When I entertain, I like the wine, beer, whiskey, sake and shochu to all flow freely—they are a great addition to a meal and help create a convivial atmosphere.

Wine is a relative newcomer to Japan. We now have our own Japanese vineyards but most people drink imported wine. Wines are very good accompaniments to Japanese meals and I do not believe that you can drink only Japanese drinks with this cuisine.

For many workers, especially men, it is a necessary part of the working day to go off to a bar and have a drink together, starting with beer and often ending with something stronger like whiskey or shochu mixed with water (mizuwari) or on the rocks. Wine in these situations is still unusual. If you join anyone Japanese for a meal or a drink, remember that it is the custom for your companion or the bar staff to pour the drinks; you should never pour for yourself.

One final thing I need to teach you is the all-important word for cheers in Japanese. It is a very simple word—kanpai! I hope you will have many opportunities to use it!

Sake

Sake is probably the most famous Japanese alcoholic drink. As it is made from rice it has a very special place in Japanese culture, and sake is drunk at important religious ceremonies such as weddings. It is also the traditional drink to celebrate the new year. Sake is made in breweries all over Japan and varies dramatically in taste, from very sweet to very dry. It is drunk in small egg cup–size cups when hot, or in regular glasses when cold. To heat sake you must first fill a small ceramic bottle, called a tokkuri, with sake and then gently warm it by placing it in a bowl of boiling water for about 5–10 minutes. Particularly in winter I really enjoy drinking my sake hot but you can have it this way any time of the year.

Beer

I may be biased but I think that Japanese beer is some of the finest in the world. Beer brewing techniques originated in Germany in the 19th century. We now produce fantastic lager-style beers, which are always served icy cold, often from a bottle. I think that beer really suits the climate of Japan and its culture. It is easy to create a party atmosphere when you are sharing a number of bottles of beer. If a group of us is celebrating, it is common to order some large bottles of beer and for everyone to have a small glass. It is not so common to order individual mugs of beer, though it is not unheard of, especially in the popular beer gardens you will often find in Japanese cities.

Shochu

Shochu is a Japanese type of spirit, which can be up to 36 percent proof, rivaling other spirits such as whiskey. In recent years shochu has gained great popularity among young Japanese, which I think shows confidence in the quality of local products in Japan. It is being promoted as a healthy type of alcohol and, because it is distilled from various grains like barley, buckwheat or millet, or even from potato, there is a huge variety of different-tasting shochu available and even bars that specialize only in shochu. I like drinking it with warm water and umeboshi or on ice with some citrus fruit, like sudachi or kabosu or even with fresh lemon.

Bento/Lunch Boxes

Bento

Any visitor to Japan will soon notice, at stations and in convenience stores, a huge range of ready-to-eat lunch boxes or, to use the Japanese word, bento. Where in the West you have a variety of fillings in sandwiches, the Japanese bento offers within one box an enormous range of tastes, textures and colors. It is an exact reflection of what usually happens at a Japanese meal, mirroring the cuisine's reliance on variety and presentation.

When my children were going to school I, like most Japanese mothers, had to get up early to prepare bento for them. Schools that do not have a cafeteria rely upon mother power to ensure that the children have good, balanced meals at lunchtime. In the same way, I often prepare a separate bento for my husband to take to his workplace. These homemade bento are often wrapped up in a large cloth like a handkerchief, ensuring that the contents are not spilled en route to school or the office.

I feel that making a bento is something rather special; it is almost like a little love letter that is opened when someone is away from home. It reminds you of home, of the person who made it for you. It is more than just food!

At the heart of most bento is rice, usually regular Japanese rice, cooked in the morning ready for the bento. However, it doesn't have to be dull. It is quite common to sprinkle different toppings on the rice, to give it extra flavor and interest. One of the most commonly used toppings is simply toasted black sesame seeds—tasty but also very attractive. You can try your own type of topping but I think something with a bit of a bite to it works best as it contrasts well with the rice. It is also common to put a red salt-pickled plum (umeboshi) on top, in the middle of the rice; it helps preserve the rice on hot summer days.

Another way of preparing the rice is to make it into rice balls called onigiri. Again, as a visitor to Japan you may see these rice balls individually wrapped for sale in convenience stores and supermarkets. They are even more like a Japanese version of a sandwich than a bento and can be made with many different types of fillings.

Here are recipes for two different kinds of fillings for rice balls—you can also create your own fillings with what you have available at the time. Refrigerate any unused fillings and use within 2–3 days.

Rice Balls

Onigiri

MAKES 2

For the tuna mayonnaise filling:

1/3 cup canned tuna

1 tablespoon mayonnaise

a little light soy sauce

For the simmered beef filling:

2/3 lb. thinly sliced beef

3½ tablespoons fresh ginger

4 tablespoons soy sauce

4 tablespoons mirin

2 tablespoons superfine sugar

2 tablespoons sake

about 1¾ cups warm cooked rice

salt and nori seaweed (optional)

1 To make the tuna mayonnaise filling: Drain the canned tuna and place in a bowl. Mix in the mayonnaise and soy sauce to taste.

2 To make the simmered beef filling: Chop the beef into bite-size pieces. Peel the ginger and slice very thinly.

3 Mix the soy sauce, mirin, sugar and sake in a pan over a medium heat. Bring to a boil, then add the beef, ensuring that the pieces do not stick together. Add the ginger and simmer until the liquid has evaporated, stirring occasionally. Leave to cool.

4 Take a large handful of warm cooked rice (between 2/3–3/4 cup). Make a hollow in the middle and place 1/2 tablespoon of the tuna mayonnaise mix inside. Close the rice around the tuna to make a ball. Sprinkle with salt. Repeat using the beef mix. You can wrap a sheet of nori seaweed around each ball, if preferred. If using the nori, do so when the rice is still warm—it will stick more easily.

So what should you put into a bento? I believe in trying to make life as easy as possible and so would suggest you look in your fridge to see what is left over from last night. Bento is a great way of using up those little bits and pieces that weren't finished off the night before. You don't need to have a lot of any one ingredient, but you do need variety of taste and texture. You also have to choose dishes that are tasty even when cold, ones that will not spoil quickly and ones that are not too watery.

It is quite common to have both meat and fish in one bento box, though one is usually more predominant than the other. Deep-fried seafood or chicken is always very popular, as is teriyaki fish or meat (see page 76).

Vegetables are crucial for a good bento. Crunchy, lightly cooked green beans, carrots or broccoli are all fantastic additions, providing color and texture. You can add a sesame dressing (see page 118) or cook them in tempura style (see page 112) to make the vegetables more of a feature. It is, of course, possible to make a bento with no meat or fish but you need to ensure that the vegetables are prepared in ways to keep the bento interesting.

Pickles, too, add to this mini banquet. They are satisfyingly crunchy and should have just enough saltiness and sourness to cut through the rice. You can make your own pickles (see page 126) and add them to your own bento.

Throughout this book, I have indicated recipes that work well in bento but really most home cooking will work. Obviously, I have my own favorite mixes. I really enjoy the combination of Ginger Pork (see page 62) and Rice with Green Peas (see page 48). It is fantastic to take the bento box lid off at lunchtime and savor the fragrance of the ginger and to feast your eyes on the green of the peas. Food should always appeal to more than just the taste buds.

In Japan there are many books specializing in bento recipes. I think the common message is to try to ensure that people don't get bored, as having the same food too often will make any meal unappetizing. Some books suggest creating pictures with the food and certainly for really young children this can be fun, though maybe not so appropriate for adults. In the same way as you plan an evening meal, it is important to get the overall picture in your mind when you are planning a bento. How do the tastes work together? Are there any contrasts of texture? Is it a healthy balance of ingredients? These are all questions you should ask yourself for almost any meal, including bento.

Just remember when you prepare a bento for someone else, you are preparing a little reminder of home. When you are making it for yourself, remember you deserve a break, so treat yourself well with a delicious, nutritious bento.

Menu Planning

Menu Planning

I am so happy to have been able to show people around the world that it is possible to cook Japanese recipes outside Japan. However, a lot of people ask me for more guidance on how and when to use these recipes and for ideas on how to serve Japanese food. I hope that in this chapter I will be able to give you some inspiration.

The main themes in Japanese food are variety and portion size, presentation and freshness. In order to eat in a more Japanese way you will need to look at these principles.

Variety & Portion Size

Many people say that Japanese food is very healthy and certainly it seems that there are not the same number of overweight people in Japan as you find in Western nations. However, I am sure you have spotted that some Japanese recipes require deep-fat frying or contain sugar. Although that might not seem very healthy I think a Japanese meal can be good for you, despite these types of dishes, because of the portion sizes and the variety present at each meal.

If you have the chance to sample many different flavors you will not need to eat so much, as you will be more satisfied. Japanese food relies heavily on this principle but I think that Asian cuisine as a whole also recognizes the importance of variety.

When you are thinking about making a meal, try to see if you can increase the number of flavors but maybe cut down on the size of the portions. It might take some time to get the right balance but I think you will enjoy it and find it a good way to eat.

Presentation

Few, if any, cuisines can match Japanese cuisine for its emphasis on presentation. I often hear my non-Japanese friends, on seeing a beautifully presented dish, say, "It looks too good to eat!" Of course, it should be eaten, but the point is that people, family, friends or guests, use their senses of smell and vision before they actually eat. To have food beautifully presented helps prepare a person to enjoy the meal.

You can use these presentation skills with any type of cuisine. You need to think about the color and shape of the food and then the plates you have. At a traditional Japanese table you would expect to see a mix of different types of ceramics, combined with some lacquer and possibly some wood or glass. We will, for example, often use a rectangular

flat plate for grilled fish, bowls for individual portions of tofu, tiny plates for pickles. The idea is for each dish to maintain its own integrity both in taste and in look; then when you eat, you have a little from each dish and so enjoy each flavor as intended.

I like to use a lot of flowers in my house and at my table. I am very fortunate to have a garden and I will try to use flowers or herbs from there, but it is also easy to buy flowers individually and you would be amazed at what you can do with just a few blooms. I always try to have some fresh flowers in the entrance hall—it creates a warm welcome. I will also use them on plates, on the table or with the cutlery or chopsticks. It doesn't have to cost a lot of money to bring your own personality to the table. Be inventive! These small touches of creativity are good for you and, I believe, help relieve the stress of everyday life.

Freshness

The most common image of Japanese food is that of sashimi or sushi. While this is not the only thing we eat, the image is close to the truth. Most food served is extremely fresh and the emphasis is very firmly on maintaining its freshness. Meat is usually served quite rare (I often have to ask for my steak to be very, very rare when I visit some foreign countries), and vegetables are prepared in a way to keep their bite.

Modern farming techniques and supermarkets have greatly increased the range of products available in and out of their normal seasons. If you love strawberries, it may be wonderful to be able to eat them all year but I think you will agree that they taste their best when they are in season, and hopefully grown locally. Despite the availability of so many things all year round, seasonality is still highly regarded in Japan. We will often design menus to highlight an ingredient that has just come into season and will decorate our tableware with reminders of the changes in the seasons.

Menus

I would like to give you some general guidelines about menus. In addition to the themes of variety, portion size and presentation, you should also consider the overall balance of the meal. For example, it would be better, from the point of view of variety, not to have more than one dish with a sesame dressing per meal. Similarly, lots of dishes using miso dressings could be overpowering if served at the same time.

Most meals work well with Japanese rice. I think that for cultures where potatoes are the main source of carbohydrates, it may be hard to imagine swapping potatoes for rice but I really recommend using Japanese rice with the meat and fish dishes in this and my previous book; you might be surprised at how tasty the result is.

Remember, you can use these recipes in isolation—or with recipes from other cuisines. For example, you can serve many of the vegetable dishes with roasted or grilled meat—it would add a new accent to any meal. You can also serve many of the meat and fish dishes with potatoes. It is worth experimenting and finding what you enjoy.

Basic Home Menus

Breakfast: Although there are people who eat cereal for breakfast in Japan, it is more traditional to have a bowl of rice, some miso soup, pickles and maybe an egg or a small piece of grilled fish. These days many Japanese will start their day with fresh salad, ham, toast, a hard-boiled egg and cheese—variety and freshness! If you go to a café in Japan you will often find they have a good value "morning set," usually a very thick slice of toast, an egg and a salad—good for people who are in a hurry.

Breakfast Menu 1
- Japanese-Style Mini Omelette, page 32
- Miso Shiru (Sesame Miso Soup Version), page 22
- Pickles, page 126

Breakfast Menu 2
- Mini Savory Steamed Egg Custards with Mushrooms, page 26
- Japanese Green Tea Risotto, page 54

Lunch: I have covered the main form of lunch in the bento section of this book but of course there are many other types of lunch too. In many towns, local restaurants will deliver to your home. This service is particularly popular when you want to eat sushi at home. As with most countries, we also have pizza delivery services—which are very popular with young Japanese.

Light Lunch Menu

- Harumi's Tuna Tataki Salad, page 93
- Miso Soup with Pork, page 24
- Rice, page 54

Vegetarian-Style Lunch Menu

- Eggplant and Harusame Noodle Salad, page 117
- Tofu with Ricotta Cheese, page 36
- Mixed Salad with Sesame Dressing, page 118
- Miso Soup with Wakame Seaweed and Potato, page 22
- Rice, page 54

Lunch Menu

- Fried Chicken with Spring Onion Sauce, page 84
- Tofu with Spicy Minced Topping, page 41
- Pickles, page 126
- Rice, page 54

Dinner: A typical dinner would consist of rice, miso shiru or another soup, pickles, a meat or fish dish, and maybe a small side dish. Alternatively, some non-Japanese dishes might be prepared; Italian, Chinese and Korean cuisines are particularly popular. Most Japanese are able to prepare recipes from all these countries. In fact, I think that the Japanese home cook is probably one of the most versatile and sophisticated cooks in the world due to the extensive range of recipes they prepare.

Dinner Menu 1

- Ginger Pork, page 62
- Miso Soup with Tofu and Wakame Seaweed, page 20
- Pickles, page 126
- Rice with Green Peas, page 48
- Baked Papaya, page 134

Dinner Menu 2

- Eggplant "Dengaku" Style, page 125
- Clear Soup with Julienne of Spring Vegetables, page 30
- Pickles, page 126
- Sea Bream on Rice, page 51

Dinner Menu 3

- Grilled Aromatic Mackerel page 97
- Miso Soup with Eggplant, page 21
- Sukiyaki Donburi, page 52

Entertaining

We love having festivals. The Japanese year is not just divided up into the four seasons but broken up by 16 national holidays and a variety of special days. In addition to national holidays such as Children's Day, New Year's Day and Respect for the Elderly Day, we celebrate nature, too, holding parties to look at the cherry blossoms or the autumn leaves. In addition, in my house we also celebrate Mother's Day, Father's Day, birthdays and wedding anniversaries. Of course, not everyone observes these events but they are part of the fabric of my country and its food and drink culture.

In Japan, the New Year festival celebrated on January 1 is a major holiday and the most important period of entertaining in the year. In my home it is a time of intense activity. Like families all over Japan, we want to have the house cleaned from top to bottom so it is fresh for the coming year. We also want to be able to relax over the three-day holiday period, so we have to buy many provisions and prepare the traditional New Year food

(called osechi ryori) before the New Year begins. This New Year cuisine is quite strong flavored and sweet, which helps preserve the food so no one has to cook for a few days. At my house, we have many visitors over the period and, although I do not have to cook very much, I am always busy—but enjoying myself.

When my children were younger I would observe many traditional Japanese festivals with them. One of my favorites was Girls' Day (March 3). Generations of Japanese women have experienced, as children, the excitement of setting up the dolls that represent the Imperial court, with the prince and princess at the top of the shelf. The family would then have a special meal, celebrating their own "princess." Boys have their own celebrations, too, but instead of dolls, tradition demands that replica samurai helmets and swords are brought out and placed on a dais for all to see.

Now that the children have grown up, as a family we only seem to celebrate a few special days. In addition to the New Year, I like to make a bit of a fuss for Valentine's Day and Christmas. In Japan, women give chocolate gifts to their husband or boyfriend on Valentine's Day. Men then have to reciprocate a month later on a day we call White Day. I think it is fun to make something like a heart-shaped chocolate fudge cake to celebrate.

Many Japanese see Christmas as an opportunity to go out as a couple; all hotels offer special Christmas entertainment and meals. In my house we prefer to have a meal at home as a family. My husband, Reiji, loves roast turkey, which we often cook for Christmas, but sometimes I like to do something different, like this pork (above), which I like to serve with Peppers and Crab Mixed Rice (see page 46) and Sautéed Bean Sprouts with Bok Choy (see page 115). It may not be traditional in Western countries but it is really delicious and makes a very special family meal.

My family likes to cook and we often entertain at home. Barbecues are popular, too. Even when we lived in a tiny apartment with a tiny yard we managed to barbecue. In fact, my husband made the furniture that we use outside—something I am still impressed by.

I hope that you will be inspired to try many of my recipes, remembering to observe the basic principles of variety and portion size, presentation and freshness. I have indicated where certain recipes combine well with others, but in many cases it will be a question of you developing your own style. Have confidence—it is not as difficult as you may think!

Glossary

If you want to ask for things in Japanese (in a shop or restaurant) it is an easy language to pronounce as long as you remember to pronounce each letter individually and to keep the vowels pure: "a" as in apple, "i" as in ink, "u" as in put, "e" as in egg and "o" as in pot. They are not accented and no sound is lengthened more than others.

Ao-nori Dried, finely chopped seaweed. Often used on top of okonomiyaki and yakisoba.

Bainiki A paste made from umeboshi (see umeboshi).

Beni Shoga A red julienned version of pickled ginger often served with okonomiyaki.

Bok choy Sometimes spelled as pak choi or bak choi. A Chinese leafy green vegetable.

Chinese soup paste A useful stock paste, tasting of a mixture of chicken and beef stock.

Daikon Japanese radish, sometimes found in Asian shops called mooli.

Dashi Stock made from kombu and dried fish flakes (katsuo bushi). The basis of much of Japanese cooking.

Gari Wafer-thin slices of pickled ginger usually served with sushi.

Harusame noodles Very fine, translucent noodles made from mung bean starch, or sometimes from sweet potato or potato starch. The name means "spring rain," which they resemble.

Kabosu A Japanese green citrus fruit.

Kamaboko A mild-flavored fish paste loaf, made from a mixture of fish flesh.

Katakuriko A potato starch similar to corn flour but stronger, so use a little more corn flour if you cannot find potato starch.

Katsuo Bushi Smoked and dried bonito fish that is shaved into very fine flakes before use. Used in many recipes, including dashi, it has a distinctive flavor.

Kikurage A tree fungus that is used more for its gelatinous texture than for flavor.

Kinome The young leaves of the sansho plant. Not readily available in the West.

Kochujan A spicy Korean miso paste.

Konnyaku A gelatinous paste made from a type of potato, either in blocks, as in oden, or in threads.

Kombu Kelp seaweed. Used to make dashi stock and in simmered foods.

La Yu Chili oil, often used with Chinese dishes like gyoza.

Mentsuyu A basic dipping sauce, usually made from dashi, soy sauce, mirin and sugar.

Mirin A sweet alcoholic liquid used in cooking to tenderize, sweeten and balance saltiness. An essential ingredient in Japanese cooking.

Miso A rich, savory paste made from fermented soy beans, salt and grain (usually rice or barley). It keeps for years and is a protein-rich addition to many dishes. It's the essential ingredient in miso soup. Red miso (akamiso) is dark and high in protein and salt. White miso (shiromiso) is milder and sweeter and suitable for dressings. Medium (awase miso) is all-purpose, being a mix of at least two types of miso.

Mitsuba Its botanical name is Cryptotaenia japonica, and it resembles flat-leaf parsley in appearance but not taste, being more aromatic and fragrant.

Mizansho An aromatic spice very similar to Szechuan pepper.

Mushrooms Japan has a huge variety of mushrooms, many of which you cannot find overseas. Most commonly used is the shiitake (dark and round—a little like chestnut mushrooms). However, maitake, shimeji, eringi and enoki are all commonly used: they differ mainly in color and thickness of the stalks. The matsutake is the most aromatic and highly valued mushroom in Japan.

Myoga The fragrant bud of a type of ginger plant, Zingiber mioga. Available pickled, but occasionally you can find the fresh bud in Asian stores. Ginger is not a substitute.

Nameko A small brown Japanese mushroom with a gelatinous coating.

Negi Japan has a huge range of vegetables from the onion family. Naga negi, banno negi, asatsuki and wakegi are the most common.

Nira Garlic chives—very pungent and tasty.

Nori Seaweed, most usually encountered as dried black, thin, crisp sheets, which are used to wrap around sushi.

Ponzu soy sauce A dipping sauce made from soy sauce and citrus juice, traditionally sudachi or yuzu, but nowadays also lemon or lime.

Rice (kome) The technical name for Japanese rice is Oryza sativa japonica. It is short grained, so it sticks together and can be eaten with chopsticks.

Rice vinegar This commonly used vinegar is made from rice and is low in acidity and mild in flavor.

Sake Japanese rice wine. Similar to a very dry sherry. Can be drunk hot or cold.

Sansho pepper Made from the ground seedpods of the prickly ash, slightly spicy with a hint of citrus. Sansho is closely related to Szechwan pepper, which is acceptable as a substitute.

Sesame oil Toasted sesame oil has a strong flavor and is used in small amounts.

Sesame paste Japanese sesame paste is rich and smooth, made from toasted sesame seeds.

Sesame seeds In Japan sesame seeds are usually sold already toasted. Both black and white sesame seeds are available.

Shichimi togarashi This is a frequently used mix of seven spices, including chili.

Shirataki noodles Fine noodles made from konnyaku, often used in sukiyaki.

Shiratamako A rice flour made from glutinous rice. It is rougher than regular flour.

Shiso Sometimes also known in Japanese as oba, or in English as perilla. It is part of the mint family though its aroma is reminiscent of basil and mint. Its leaves look rather like nettle leaves. It is used as a garnish with sashimi, or chopped and served with rice or in salads.

Shochu A colorless spirit distilled from grain or starch, such as potato, barley or millet.

Shokoshu A Chinese rice wine that has a stronger flavor than sake with a subtle undertone of herbs. A dry sherry is a reasonable substitute.

Shungiku Edible leaves from the spring chrysanthemum.

Soy sauce Made from soybeans, wheat and salt, soy sauce is the ubiquitous flavoring in Japanese cooking. The regular soy sauce (koikuchi) is readily available in the West. A thinner soy sauce (usukuchi) is lighter, but actually saltier, and used when you don't want to darken the appearance of the food too much.

Sudachi A small, pale yellow citrus fruit.

To-Ban-Jan Chinese chili paste.

Tofu A curd made from coagulated soy milk. There are two main types of fresh tofu: soft or silken tofu (kinugoshidofu). This falls apart easily and is best eaten just as it is with soy sauce and ginger, but it's also good for dips and dressings. Firm or cotton tofu (momendofu) is the pressed curds and therefore firmer. This is good for cooking.

Udo One of the few vegetables native to Japan. It has a distinctive aroma and texture. Good in spring.

Umeboshi A salt-pickled apricot. It can be small and hard or large and soft.

Wakame A mild and delicate seaweed. Available dried, it quickly rehydrates and is a common addition to miso soup and salads.

Wakegi A member of the onion family, widely available in spring.

Wasabi The ground root of what is often referred to as "Japanese horseradish." This is the green paste served with sashimi and sushi. Extremely pungent, it can be bought in tubes, or as a powder ready to mix with water.

Yuzu A Japanese citrus fruit used in many traditional Japanese recipes.

Zaa sai Chinese green crunchy pickles. They are very salty and need to be rinsed before use. They add a certain richness of taste when used in cooking.

Sources

In addition to local Japanese and Asian food markets, the Internet offers an array of sources for hard-to-find ingredients. Below are just a few suggestions.

Amazon.com
www.amazon.com/kitchens
Asian foods and cooking equipment

Asian Food Grocer
www.asianfoodgrocer.com
Asian foods

Eden Foods
www.edenfoods.com
Asian foods

Joyce Chen Products
www.joycechen.com
Asian foods and cooking equipment

Kalustyan's
www.kalustyans.com
800-352-3451
Asian and other specialty ingredients

Kitazawa Seed Co.
P.O. Box 13220
Oakland, CA 94661
510-595-1188
510-595-1860 fax
Asian and other seeds